THE TUDORS

A ROYAL HISTORY OF ENGLAND

THE TUDORS

BY NEVILLE WILLIAMS

EDITED BY
ANTONIA FRASER

University of California Press
Berkeley   Los Angeles

University of California Press
Berkeley and Los Angeles, California

Published by arrangement with Cassell & Co

The text of *The Tudors* is taken from the single-volume
The Lives of the Kings & Queens of England, first published in the United Kingdom in 1975 by
Weidenfeld & Nicolson, revised in 1993 and 1998.

Cataloging-in-Publication data is on file with the Library of Congress.

ISBN 0-520-22804-9

Jacket images: front © The Bridgeman Art Library, London (the Court of Wards and Liveries,
c. 1598); back © AKG London (portrait of Elizabeth I by Marcus Geeraerts the Younger).

Endpapers: 'A Palace Interior with Ladies and Gentlemen Dancing and Playing Music' by
Louis de Caullery. *Page 2*: Portrait of Edward VI from the studio of William Scrots.

Printed and bound in Italy.
9 8 7 6 5 4 3 2 1

CONTENTS

INTRODUCTION

The Wars of the Roses and the battle between the Houses of Lancaster and York that had raged for the duration of Henry VI's reign and that of Edward IV and Richard III resolved itself with the eventual union of the two houses. In 1486, Henry VII, son of Edmund Tudor and Margaret Beaufort, married Elizabeth of York, daughter of Edward IV. The Tudor dynasty was established. The Middle Ages fought their way to a finish and, although Henry Tudor's claim to the throne was somewhat 'patchy', he succeeded in laying down the guidelines of Tudor despotism for his powerful royal descendants: the dazzling Henry VIII and the glorious Elizabeth I. With the end of the wars of the nobility that had bedevilled and crippled England in the past centuries, medieval kingship gave way to heraldic pageantry and sumptuous monarchy. The reign of the House of Tudor was also the period that saw the spread of new religious thinking – thinking that was to radically affect both the monarchy and the constitution.

The larger-than-life figure of Henry VIII straddles the stage of English history. In him we seem to have the very pattern of majesty, the role of the monarch as it should be played in an age when outward kingly attributes were all-important. In the first years of his reign, Henry was a prodigy of intelligence, energy, even beauty. A strong claim to being the best known of our monarchs, he is also one of England's most controversial. His splendid reign eventually gave way to a blood-stained sunset: the execution of Thomas More, the people's tragedy of the Pilgrimage of Grace, the terrible fates of his wives. Quite apart from the marital junketings with which we are all familiar, Henry's importance in English history is immeasurable, since his reign contains the beginnings of the Reformation and the exchange of an international Church subordinate to Rome for a State Church under the headship of the King.

Henry VIII's young son by Jane Seymour, Edward VI, ascended to the throne in 1547 when he was only ten years old. At a time of acute political and religious controversy, of execution and exile, the young king was inevitably surrounded by a circle of powerful advisors. With the penning of the first version of the English Common Prayer Book in 1549 by Archbishop Thomas Cranmer, Catholic ceremony, paraphernalia and idolatry were abolished and England was 'declared' Protestant. But the new religion was precarious and, at the death of the sickly young boy-king in 1553, the crown passed to his fanatical, Catholic half-sister, Mary.

The story of Mary Tudor constitutes one of the most poignant chapters in the history of English monarchy. She saw her own mother, Catherine of Aragon, cruelly discarded and with this her own right to the succession dismissed. She then married King Philip II of Spain, whom she loved but who did not love her and, despite all her frantic prayers, she could not bear children. And neither did she, during her short five-year reign, manage to achieve the goal on which she had set her heart: the return of her subjects to allegiance to the Church of Rome. Instead, she united her subjects in their hatred of Rome and blackened her own reputation before posterity. The first female sovereign to reign since Matilda, Mary's rule was regarded as an example of the sort of failure which a woman on the throne was always bound to produce. Such prejudice, however, was to be radically overturned as soon as the crown passed to Mary's Protestant half-sister, Elizabeth.

'You may well have a greater prince, but you shall never have a more loving prince.' So declared Elizabeth I in December 1558 on the defeat of the Spanish Armada. There are many indeed who still feel that England shall never have a 'greater prince' let alone a more loving one than Queen Elizabeth, the Virgin Queen. The impression she conveyed was that she loved her English people, and this made her unique among sovereigns. The concept of a queen wedded to her subjects was brilliantly and expertly expressed in her life style: her bridegroom remained the English people during her long reign, from 1558 to 1603. Was this indeed the truth, or is it that Elizabeth was the supreme calculating exponent of the public image, manipulating femininity to her cool advantage? Whatever the answer may be, Elizabeth successfully ruled in an age of intense and fierce religious controversy and negotiated her way to become the first monarch to bestow her name upon an age. It is our feeling of certainty that her reign was a success, combined with our uncertainty about the personality of Elizabeth herself, that have ensured that we continue to be as enthralled today by the Virgin Queen and her Golden Age, as our ancestors were.

THE TUDORS
1485-1603

HENRY VII 1485-1509
HENRY VIII 1509-47
EDWARD VI 1547-53
MARY I 1553-8
ELIZABETH 1558-1603

Opposite: A coin struck to commemorate the marriage of Henry VII to Elizabeth of York in 1486. Their marriage was aimed at uniting the rival houses of York and Lancaster. The tall, golden-haired Elizabeth was a renowned beauty, and Henry was deeply affected when Elizabeth died in childbed in 1503.

THE TUDORS AND STUARTS

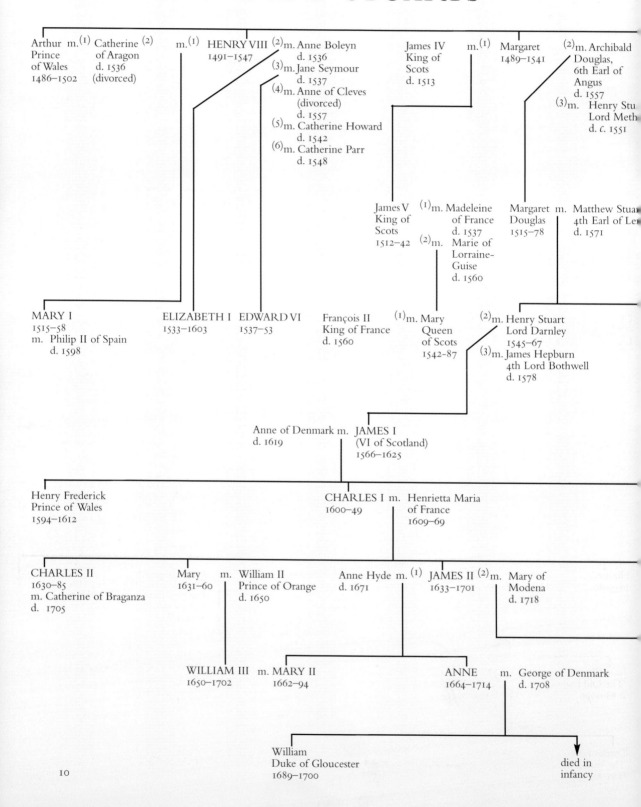

Arthur m.(1) Catherine (2) m.(1) HENRY VIII (2)m. Anne Boleyn   James IV   m.(1) Margaret   (2)m. Archibald
Prince   of Aragon   1491–1547   d. 1536   King of   1489–1541   Douglas,
of Wales   d. 1536   (3)m. Jane Seymour   Scots   6th Earl of
1486–1502   (divorced)   d. 1537   d. 1513   Angus
                                                 (4)m. Anne of Cleves   d. 1557
                                                     (divorced)   (3)m. Henry Stu
                                                     d. 1557   Lord Meth
                                                 (5)m. Catherine Howard   d. c. 1551
                                                     d. 1542
                                                 (6)m. Catherine Parr
                                                     d. 1548

                                                    James V   (1)m. Madeleine   Margaret   m. Matthew Stua
                                                    King of   of France   Douglas   4th Earl of Le
                                                    Scots   d. 1537   1515–78   d. 1571
                                                    1512–42   (2)m. Marie of
                                                                   Lorraine-
                                                                   Guise
                                                                   d. 1560

MARY I   ELIZABETH I   EDWARD VI   François II   (1)m. Mary   (2)m. Henry Stuart
1515–58   1533–1603   1537–53   King of France   Queen   Lord Darnley
m. Philip II of Spain   d. 1560   of Scots   1545–67
    d. 1598   1542–87   (3)m. James Hepburn
                                                                                              4th Lord Bothwell
                                                                                              d. 1578

                        Anne of Denmark m. JAMES I
                            d. 1619   (VI of Scotland)
                                            1566–1625

Henry Frederick   CHARLES I m. Henrietta Maria
Prince of Wales   1600–49   of France
1594–1612   1609–69

CHARLES II   Mary   m. William II   Anne Hyde m. (1) JAMES II (2)m. Mary of
1630–85   1631–60   Prince of Orange   d. 1671   1633–1701   Modena
m. Catherine of Braganza   d. 1650   d. 1718
d. 1705

            WILLIAM III m. MARY II   ANNE   m. George of Denmark
            1650–1702   1662–94   1664–1714   d. 1708

                            William   died in
                            Duke of Gloucester   infancy
                            1689–1700

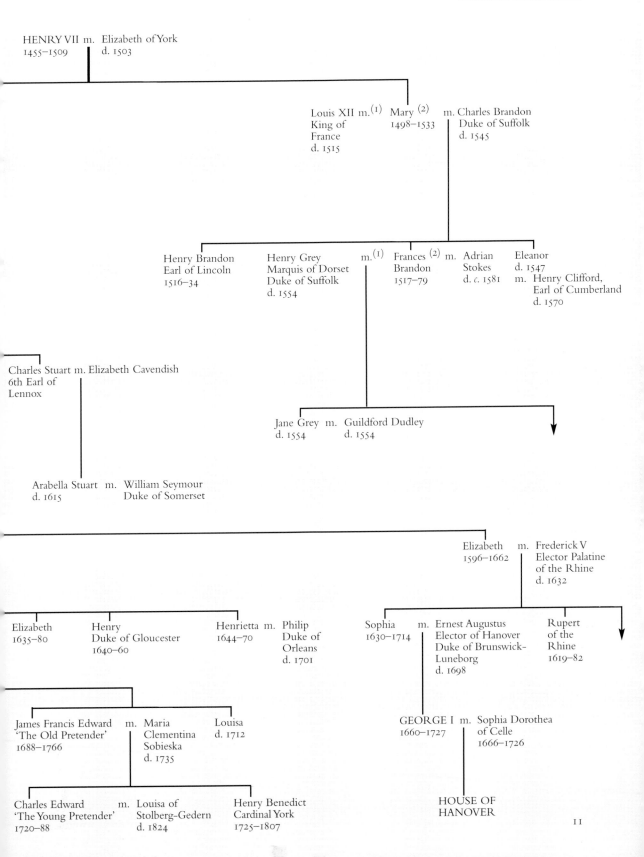

HENRY VII m. Elizabeth of York
1455–1509   d. 1503

Louis XII m.(1) Mary (2) m. Charles Brandon
King of   1498–1533   Duke of Suffolk
France   d. 1545
d. 1515

Henry Brandon   Henry Grey   m.(1) Frances (2) m. Adrian   Eleanor
Earl of Lincoln   Marquis of Dorset   Brandon   Stokes   d. 1547
1516–34   Duke of Suffolk   1517–79   d. c. 1581 m. Henry Clifford,
                     d. 1554   Earl of Cumberland
                                                                              d. 1570

Charles Stuart m. Elizabeth Cavendish
6th Earl of
Lennox

                                            Jane Grey m. Guildford Dudley
                                            d. 1554   d. 1554

Arabella Stuart m. William Seymour
d. 1615   Duke of Somerset

                                                          Elizabeth   m. Frederick V
                                                          1596–1662   Elector Palatine
                                                                          of the Rhine
                                                                          d. 1632

Elizabeth   Henry   Henrietta m. Philip   Sophia   m. Ernest Augustus   Rupert
1635–80   Duke of Gloucester 1644–70   Duke of   1630–1714   Elector of Hanover   of the
             1640–60   Orleans   Duke of Brunswick-   Rhine
                                             d. 1701   Luneborg   1619–82
                                                                       d. 1698

James Francis Edward m. Maria   Louisa   GEORGE I   m. Sophia Dorothea
'The Old Pretender'   Clementina   d. 1712   1660–1727   of Celle
1688–1766   Sobieska   1666–1726
                          d. 1735

Charles Edward   m. Louisa of   Henry Benedict   HOUSE OF
'The Young Pretender'   Stolberg-Gedern Cardinal York   HANOVER
1720–88   d. 1824   1725–1807   11

THE ARMS OF HENRY VII AND HENRY VIII

THE FIRST KING SERIOUSLY AND consistently to use supporters was Henry VII. He favoured the dragon and greyhound. The dragon was associated with Cadwalader, the last native ruler of Britain, from whom Henry claimed descent. Certainly it was a favourite of the first Tudor King, who used it freely as a badge and motif in decoration and even created a new pursuivant (a junior herald) and named him Rouge Dragon.

The greyhound appears to have been a badge or beast associated with the House of Lancaster, from which line came Henry VII's drop of royal blood, his mother being a great-granddaughter of John of Gaunt, Duke of Lancaster. It was later associated with the earldom of Richmond and Henry VII's father, Edmund Tudor, used it as a supporter after being created Earl of Richmond. Although there are examples of early mottoes, Henry VII was the first king to use the motto *Dieu et mon droit* ('God and my right') more or less consistently. For this reason it has been shown in the illustration. The archaic spelling of *droict* has been used below.

In the illustration of Henry's arms it will be seen that the shield is the fluted and scalloped tilting shield. There is no significance in this except that it was fashionable at the time. Arms may be shown on any shape of shield, just as the mantling may be drawn in any way the artist pleases. In heraldry only the actual objects (called charges), their disposition and colour remain unalterable.

The other coat illustrated here is that of Henry VIII. He sometimes used a greyhound supporter but preferred the crowned lion of England; for it must not be forgotten that the Lancastrians and the Beauforts would have had less significance for the son of the heiress of the House of York, for Henry's mother Elizabeth was Edward IV's eldest daughter.

Henry VIII was the first monarch consistently to use a crown of crosses formy and fleurs-de-lys with arches. There are some representations of his father's arms ensigned with such a crown but Henry and succeeding sovereigns always used it.

They also encircled their arms with the insignia of the Order of the Garter; a blue garter garnished with gold and embroidered with the motto of the Order *Honi soit qui mal y pense* ('Evil to him who evil thinks').

THE ARMS OF PHILIP
AND ELIZABETH I

EDWARD VI AND MARY I, UNTIL HER marriage, used the same arms as their father. After Mary's marriage half of Philip's complex quartered coat was placed side by side with the quartered royal arms on a single shield supported by Philip's black eagle crowned with a golden crown and a lion of England, for it must be remembered that Philip was King of England although he had to demit his regal powers when Mary died childless.

As the illustration shows, Philip's arms were divided into four grand quarters so that when just the two on the left-hand side were shown conjoined to Mary's arms no symbolism was lost. The first and last grand quarters are the castle of Castile and lion of Leon quartered and repeated. Side by side in the other quarters are the coats of Aragon and Sicily. In the second and third grand quarters are four coats, namely Austria (the white band on red), Burgundy modern (the French royal arms with a border), Burgundy ancient and the lion of Brabant. Over all is a shield on which the lion of Flanders is shown side by side with the eagle of Tyrol. The pomegranate in the point in base symbolises Granada.

Elizabeth I, whose arms are shown beneath Philip's, added an extra touch of splendour to the royal arms. She adopted a gold barred helmet facing outward and substituted a gold for a red mantling. From her reign onwards this helm and mantling have been a coveted privilege of royalty. Queen Elizabeth also affected her own motto *Semper eadem* ('Always the same').

Badges, unlike arms, were usually simple devices employed to mark retainers and property. They also appeared on the long rallying flag, the standard. In the Middle Ages the badge was more often associated with a place than a person or family. The royal family, having vast possessions, have used a multiplicity of badges. The Tudor rose, crowned thistle, white boar and gold portcullis are among the best known.

The badges illustrated are the falcon badge, which was a favourite badge of Elizabeth and had been previously used by her mother Anne Boleyn, and the crowned Tudor rose. This famous badge symbolised the coming together of the Houses of York and Lancaster in the Tudor dynasty. It was used by all the Tudors and, uncrowned, has remained a popular heraldic symbol.

HENRY VII *r.* 1485–1509

THOUGH IT DID NOT SEEM SO at the time, 22 August 1485 remains a seminal date in the history of English monarchy, for it ushered in the House of Tudor and, ever since, the Crown of England has remained in the line of the heirs of Henry Tudor, the victor at Bosworth Field. A dynasty was born. Henry was head of the House of Lancaster through his remarkable mother, Margaret Beaufort, and he soon strengthened his claim to the throne of England by Parliamentary approval and by his marriage with Elizabeth of York who was destined to bear him three sons and four daughters, though only their second son, Henry, and their eldest and third daughters, Margaret and Mary respectively, were to survive their parents. Henry VIII was to become so desperate to beget a healthy male heir that he divorced his first wife to the consternation of Christendom and beheaded the second before embarking on four further marriages, the last three of them childless, and left, like his father, a son and two daughters. These all died without issue, yet their combined reigns lasted from 1547 to 1603, when James VI of Scotland, great-grandson of Henry VII's daughter Margaret, came south to inaugurate the rule of the House of Stuart. Such was a notable legacy of the first Tudor, who throughout his reign was haunted by the fear that an army no larger than the one which he had himself led against Richard III might overthrow him. His son too was threatened by Yorkist pretenders and his grandchildren troubled by rival claimants of 'the blood royal', yet they all died in their beds. The principle of legitimacy had triumphed.

The only son of Edmund Tudor, Earl of Richmond, and Lady Margaret Beaufort, the future Henry VII was very much a child of the

Opposite: A sixteenth-century bust of Henry VII attributed to Pietro Torrigiano and made of painted gesso on wood.

civil wars of Lancaster and York, for his father had been taken by the Yorkists in the summer of 1456 and died a prisoner in Carmarthen Castle, leaving a widow of no more than thirteen years who pinned her hopes on giving birth to a son. Edmund's brother, Jasper Tudor, Earl of Pembroke, brought Margaret to his stronghold of Pembroke Castle, where Henry was born on 28 January 1457. In after years when he had achieved all her ambitions for him, she would write to him on his birthday, 'This day of St Agnes, that I did bring into this world my good and gracious prince'; but before then there were to be many tribulations. Henry was only four when, following Edward IV's seizure of the Crown in 1461, Pembroke fell to the Yorkists and mother and child were placed under the guardianship of William Herbert, the new owner, who was granted Jasper's earldom, while Jasper himself fled abroad. Henry was now parted from his mother, who married a Lancastrian knight, Sir Henry Stafford, but he received a sound schooling and was intended as a husband for Herbert's daughter.

When he was twelve his guardian was executed for alleged treason by Warwick, the Kingmaker, yet the following year, when Henry VI was restored to his throne, Jasper could return from exile and bring his nephew to the Lancastrian court. Henry VI, seeing the youth from Wales for the first time, greeted him, 'This truly, this is he unto whom both we and our adversaries much yield and give over the dominion.' Those were prophetic words, for within a year the King had died, his own line became extinct and the young Henry Tudor became the true heir of the House of Lancaster. Edward IV recovered the Crown at the battle of Barnet on Easter Day 1471, and as it was no longer safe for Henry and his uncle to remain even in wild Wales they found political asylum in north-west France, which then formed the independent Duchy of Brittany. Henry was destined to stay here for fourteen impressionable years. We know little about his exile, though by all accounts he was tall for a Welshman, and if his hair was dark he had a fair complexion; he was athletic and rode well.

What was the strength of Henry's claim to the throne? On his father's side it was weak. His grand-father, Owen Tudor, had secretly married Catherine of Valois, widow of Henry V, and when Henry VI came of age his step-father and his half-brothers, Edmund and Jasper Tudor, were high in favour, until civil war broke out in 1461. On his mother's side the claim went much deeper, for her great-grandfather was John of Gaunt, who had a number of children by his mistress,

Opposite: The remarkable Lady Margaret Beaufort, mother of Henry VII and wife of Edmund Tudor, Earl of Richmond. In accordance with her will, St John's College, Cambridge, was founded in 1511.

Catherine Swynford, who were subsequently legitimised; they were known as Beauforts, after Beaufort Castle in France where they were brought up. The second boy, Henry Beaufort, became a cardinal and for a time ruler of England, but the elder boy was created Earl of Somerset, and his own son John, who came to the earldom, left at his death a daughter of three years, Margaret Beaufort, who ten years later gave birth to Henry Tudor. With the deaths of both Henry VI and his son Prince Edward in 1471, Henry Tudor became head of the House of Lancaster. As such, he was a potential threat to the Yorkist regime, and Edward IV made various attempts to lay hands on him.

Richard III's usurpation of the throne in June 1483 had antagonised many of the Yorkist nobility and subsequent rumours of the murders of Edward V and his brother brought Henry appreciably nearer the throne. Later that year the Duke of Buckingham had prematurely staged a rebellion in favour of Henry, which was easily suppressed, though the conspirators who escaped from England came to swell Henry's tiny court in exile. He took a solemn oath in Rennes Cathedral at Christmas 1483 that once he became King of England he would marry Princess Elizabeth, heiress of the House of York. His greatest asset was his Welsh blood and the bards fervently proclaimed his just cause, so that when he landed in Pembrokeshire in August 1485, he attracted a large following. His army marched north via Shrewsbury and thence to Stafford and Tamworth to face Richard III south-west of Market Bosworth in Leicestershire. Only nine peers had answered Richard's summons but they included Howard of Norfolk. It was Henry's good fortune to have the support of Oxford, a most experienced soldier, while Richard found himself deserted by Northumberland. As Richard rode down Ambien Hill with his household knights to charge at Henry's bodyguards, he was surrounded by Stanley's horsemen and toppled from his horse to death. In a brief engagement, Henry became master of the realm.

Henry's weak claim to the Crown was of small moment compared with the outcome of the day's fighting. He had accepted the invitation of Richard's rebellious subjects to put his claim to the test of trial by battle, and had slain the reigning King. Without doubt, he was *de facto* sovereign and on the last day of October was crowned in Westminster Abbey. Eight days later Parliament assembled to greet him as a second Joshua, sent to rescue his people from tyranny, and an Act was speedily passed declaring the inheritance of the Crown to have come as of right to Henry and the heirs of his body. Pope Innocent VIII subsequently threatened any who

challenged his legitimate kingship with excommunication. Early in 1486 Henry married Elizabeth to unite the rival houses.

Elizabeth was eight years younger than her husband and a woman of considerable beauty. She was tall, of fair complexion with long golden tresses, and her funeral effigy indicates most graceful features. There was no role for her to play in politics beyond becoming Henry's Queen and the mother of his children. By contrast, her mother, the Queen Dowager Elizabeth Woodville, was a mischievous woman and Henry suspected her of being thick with the Yorkist conspirators in 1486, so he persuaded her to withdraw to Bermondsey Abbey, a religious house to which kings of England had the right to present their relatives. Her dower lands were settled on Elizabeth of York; she died in 1492 and was buried at Windsor beside Edward IV.

The marriage of Henry VII and Elizabeth of York, 18 January 1486, united the houses at the centre of Wars of the Roses.

Henry's consort was gentle and devout in the tradition of the great ladies of medieval chivalric poetry, and brought out the best in her husband. After years of exile – almost his whole life until his accession – he had a settled home and a growing family. The moral laxity of continental courts was a byword, yet Henry remained faithful to Elizabeth. Theirs had been a political marriage, not a love match, but they grew together; he came to show her exceptional tenderness and consoled her in a most moving way when their eldest child tragically died in 1502. When, the following year, she died in childbed, Henry was stricken with grief and 'privily departed to a solitary place and would no man should resort unto him'. Thomas More wrote an elegy in which the dying Queen addresses her husband:

Adieu! Mine own dear spouse, my worthy lord!
The faithful love, that did us both continue
In marriage and peaceable concord,
Into your hands here I do resign,
To be bestowed on your children and mine;
Erst were ye father, now must ye supply
The mother's part also, for here I lie.

Until then, domestic happiness, with the future of the Tudor dynasty assured, had enabled Henry to weather the storms of internal disaffection and foreign intrigue.

In September 1486 Henry had chosen Winchester, the ancient capital of Saxon England, for Elizabeth's lying-in and here she was delivered of a son who was named Arthur 'in honour of the British race'. He was hailed as a prince who would inaugurate a golden age, this scion equally of Lancaster and York, and heir to a united England and a unified Wales. Whom he married was to be of fundamental importance. As early as 1489 Henry planned that Arthur should be betrothed to Catherine of Aragon, the daughter of Ferdinand and Isabella of Spain. It was recognition of England's new status that he should succeed in allying his family with those powerful sovereigns of Aragon and Castile and, despite the perils of diplomacy and mutual suspicion of the two Kings, a marriage treaty was ultimately signed so that Catherine left Spain for good and landed in Plymouth in October 1501. Anxious until he had set eyes on his son's bride, Henry was delighted with the graceful Princess and Arthur declared that 'no woman in the world could be more agreeable'. They were married in St Paul's Cathedral and, after a month of court celebrations, set out for Ludlow; yet here in March the Prince of Wales and hope of England died of consumption in his sixteenth year.

Margaret had been born in 1489 and, two years later, another son, Henry, Duke of York, who was intended for the Church, but Margaret and Mary (born in 1495) were expected in that age of matrimonial diplomacy to marry into royal houses to strengthen England's alliances. Princess Margaret was to marry James IV of Scotland at Holyrood House in 1503, an event celebrated by William Dunbar in his poem, *The Thistle and the Rose*, which prophesied in a mysterious way the union of the Crowns of the two warring kingdoms which would come about exactly one hundred years later, when James VI travelled south to succeed Elizabeth I. The younger Princess, Mary, was to be the subject of a series of conflicting treaties of betrothal, but remained single until 1514.

To the end of his reign Henry was troubled by Yorkist claimants to the throne and by pretenders. Immediately after his victory at Bosworth he had sent to the Tower of London the ten-year-old Earl of Warwick (the son of Edward IV's brother, the Duke of Clarence) for he was the chief Yorkist competitor, yet King Henry could not feel secure until another claimant, John de la Pole, Earl of Lincoln, who had fled from the battlefield, was also in custody. In the autumn of 1486, not long after Arthur's birth, came disturbing news of a pretender, claiming to be the young Warwick, who, it was rumoured, had escaped from the Tower. Lambert Simnel, who had been carefully groomed for this impersonation, swiftly became the hope of the White Rose and even those, such as Lincoln, who were satisfied that Simnel was an imposter saw him as a useful puppet. With aid from Margaret of Burgundy, an implacable foe of Henry's, there seemed enough support for the Plantagenet cause 'to give the King's grace a breakfast'. Once the conspirators had toppled the throne, Simnel could be cast aside either for the real Warwick, if he were still alive, or for Lincoln himself. Lincoln and Francis Lovell were able to hire 2,000 German mercenaries as the nucleus of an army, which sailed to Ireland where Simnel was crowned 'Edward VI' on White Sunday 1487. (Long afterwards Henry mocked an Irish delegation by saying, 'My lords of Ireland, you will crown apes at last.') Yet in 1487 the threat seemed very real when the rebels landed in Lancashire and made their way towards the heart of England, for the King had no standing army and no mercenaries. But at the battle of

Stoke the pretender's army was routed, Lincoln slain and Lovell drowned while attempting to escape. Simnel received unexpected clemency, for he was put to work as a turn-spit in the royal kitchen.

The White Rose did not, however, die at Stoke, for there was soon to be another impostor, Master Perkin Warbeck from Tournai, whom the men of Cork felt convinced was Richard of York, the younger of the Princes in the Tower. His cause was soon supported by the Kings of France and Scotland, by Margaret of Burgundy and by the Emperor Maximilian, all of them anxious to embarrass Henry Tudor. The King at first made derisory comments about 'this lad who calls himself Plantagenet', yet Perkin Warbeck was to trouble him for six years. After Lincoln's treachery, Henry felt he could trust no one and his minute inquiries established that Sir William Stanley and others in high places were prepared to throw in their lot with the pretender. Their execution took the heart out of the Yorkist disaffection and when Warbeck landed at Deal in Kent, he found no supporters, so he sailed on, first to Ireland, and then to Scotland, where he was fêted at court. The large-scale invasion of England planned by James IV degenerated into a border raid, yet Henry was bent on humbling the Scots and forcing the surrender of Warbeck, so he summoned Parliament to vote heavy war taxation.

The men of Cornwall resisted the collection of the subsidy and under Michael Joseph, a smith, and Thomas Flamank, a lawyer, raised an army, it was said, of 15,000 men to march on London and force Henry to dismiss his financial ministers, Archbishop Morton and Sir Reginald Bray, who had advised him 'to pill and poll the people'. Lord Audley agreed to lead the Cornish rebels who made their way across England to camp on Blackheath. On 17 June 1497 they were defeated by the royalist troops under Lord Daubeney. Joseph, Flamank and Audley were executed, but the rest were pardoned on condition they returned peaceably to Cornwall.

The problem of Perkin Warbeck remained. Henry sent an embassy to James IV to demand his surrender, but the pretender had already left by the west coast; instead of making straight for Cornwall he foolishly wasted precious weeks in Ireland and did not land in England until early September. For a time Henry looked like having to fight on two fronts, but when James crossed the border to begin the siege of Norham Castle he was repelled by a massive force under the Earl of Surrey and speedily agreed to a truce. In Bodmin, meanwhile, Warbeck had himself proclaimed 'Richard IV' and attracted a strong following. Exeter resisted

Opposite: Margaret Tudor, daughter of Henry VII. Her marriage to James IV of Scotland in 1503 was intended to strengthen Henry's diplomatic position.

the rebels, but they made for Taunton where the pretender learned that the King's army was only twenty miles off. In panic he tried to find a boat in Southampton Water, but the coast was too well guarded, so he threw himself on Henry's mercy. As with Simnel, Henry showed great clemency and only required Perkin to reside at court, but when he abused his freedom he was sent to the Tower. In 1499 there were rash plans to rescue his fellow prisoner, Warwick, and Henry decided he would take no further chances; both Warbeck and the Earl of Warwick were executed. It is hard to acquit the King of the charge of judicial murder over the latter's end, for Warwick had been a close prisoner since the accession and was guilty of no crime beyond his Yorkist blood.

Even with Warwick out of the way, Henry still felt uneasy, because Edmund de la Pole, Earl of Suffolk, the brother of Lincoln, had picked up the Yorkist gauntlet as the century closed and fled abroad to seek help from the Emperor Maximilian. Eventually in 1506 Henry succeeded in forcing the Archduke Philip to send him back to England and 'the White Rose of England' was confined in the Tower until seven years later, when he was summarily executed by Henry VIII.

Henry Tudor's dynastic success was exemplified by two buildings, Richmond Palace and his chapel at Westminster Abbey. The small palace of Sheen in Surrey, by the River Thames, named after the Old English word for a beauty spot, had been a favourite residence of Edward III and Henry found it a pleasant retreat from London. He planned to keep Christmas here in 1498, but a few days before the palace was seriously damaged by fire and, surveying the ruins, he decided to replace Sheen manor with a splendid residence in the Gothic style, built round a paved courtyard. Within two years the new building was ready for occupation. The privy lodging for the royal family was decorated with fourteen turrets and it boasted an exceptional number of windows, yet the main architectural feature was a great tower. To crown his achievement Henry gave the palace a new name – Richmond – which perpetuated the title of the earldom and honour of Richmond in Yorkshire, which had been his until he became King. Richmond Palace was to become a favourite residence of both Henry VIII and Elizabeth I.

Despite the union of the Red Rose with the White, depicted in the emblem of 'The Tudor Rose' worn by the Yeomen of the Guard which he had established, Henry was at pains to emphasise his own Lancastrian heritage by glorifying the name of the martyred King Henry VI who had predicted his own triumphant accession.

Portrait of Perkin Warbeck, pretender to the English throne. Warbeck, supported by many of Henry VII's enemies, claimed he was Richard of York. After a failed attempt to usurp the crown Warbeck surrendered himself to Henry and was executed in 1499.

Accordingly he decided to enlarge Westminster Abbey, pulling down the Lady Chapel behind the high altar to make way for an impressive new chapel to house a shrine to Henry VI. Negotiations were opened with the Pope for a formal pronouncement on the claim for the King's canonisation, by submitting evidence about miracles performed at his tomb, though the affair had made little progress by 1509. There was also an unseemly dispute between the canons of St George's, Windsor, and the monks of Chertsey and of Westminster about the custody of the relics of Henry VI, for the offerings of pilgrims at important shrines added significantly to a monastery's income. In the end Henry's coffin remained at Windsor. Work on the memorial chapel at Westminster had been going steadily forward since 1503 and Henry had drawn up an elaborate series of foundation statutes for what had in effect become his own chapel. The stately proportions of the building owed much to Sir Reginald Bray's plans, but it was not to be completed until 1519 by the master mason Robert Vertue. In his will Henry charged his executors with the task of commissioning a sculptor to work on the tombs of his wife, his mother and himself and, as a result, the Florentine Pietro Torrigiano was invited to England to execute these monuments with their life-like effigies.

Overlooking Henry's tomb is a carving of the red dragon of Wales, which had been his personal standard in 1483. He had recognised the importance of paying due honour to his Welsh heritage in a way which would satisfy the ambitions of the men from the principality who had been swayed by the Anglophobia of the bards to rise for 'Richmond's cause'. Some of them later complained that after Bosworth Field there had been no vengeance meted out to the English foe and though minor posts were found at court for a number of Welshmen, and Rhys ap Thomas of Dynevor – affectionately called 'Father Rhys' by the King – was given the Garter, Henry had no wish to revive the troublesome Marcher lordships which had so weakened the Crown in the Wars of the Roses. The government of South Wales he left to his uncle Jasper and when he died without heirs, his extensive chain of lordships passed to the Crown. To give the Welsh people pride in the Tudor dynasty Henry created Arthur Prince of Wales and on his marriage he was sent to keep his court at Ludlow, where he received the homage of the Griffiths, Vaughans and Herberts, whose families were to provide the backbone of local government. Henry had become a thoroughly 'English' King and resisted all moves for Welsh vengeance across the Marches. Indeed he began a series of reforms which foreshadowed the Act of 1536 for incorporating Wales into the English administrative and legal system.

Henry VII was much less of an innovator than was once thought, for he built on the foundations of Yorkist experiments in autocratic, efficient government and there was much continuity in the servants of both regimes. But although he did not create the 'new monarchy' in England, he certainly strengthened the Crown's power and succeeded in taming the great landed aristocracy so that his writs ran throughout the realm. The Lancastrians had a reputation for financial incompetence, but Henry knew the importance of exploiting the Crown's revenues. He had set out to make himself solvent as the surest way of keeping his throne, and he audited accounts himself. He took a keen interest in trade, especially with

Opposite: A portrait, *c.* 1499, of Arthur, Prince of Wales, named 'in honour of the English race', who carried on his young shoulders hopes for a golden age for the kingdom. He died of consumption at the age of fifteen.

The Venetian navigator and cartographer Sebastian Cabot. Henry VII provided financial support for Cabot's voyages of exploration to Newfoundland.

the Netherlands, where the great port of Antwerp was the unrivalled centre of European trade, and through his commercial treaties secured special privileges for the English Merchant Adventurers. He also financed the Cabots' voyages of exploration to Newfoundland. As he became fully aware of his strength he cowed the baronage by fines and bonds. Perhaps in re-establishing royal power and a strong administration he had pressed too hard, for once he was gone his key ministers, Empson and Dudley, were thrown to the wolves.

After Elizabeth's death Henry became almost a recluse and his court a sombre place. He seemed prematurely an old man, yet was reluctant to instruct Prince Henry in the science of government. To the end he was fearful that those foxy diplomatists the Emperor Maximilian and King Ferdinand of Spain might outwit him, and yet he seemed more of a pilgrim, seeking a crown of glory in the next world, in the tradition of the medieval Church, with his obsession for his new foundation at Westminster Abbey. Although he was never popular, when he died in April 1509, aged fifty-two, Henry Tudor had brought internal peace and prosperity to England and given her a reputation in Europe she had not enjoyed for a century.

The gilt-bronze effigy of Elizabeth of York, which lies next to that of Henry VII on their black marble tomb in Westminster Abbey. Created by the Florentine sculptor Pietro Torrigiano, who was brought to England to execute the instructions of Henry's will, the tomb is the first Renaissance monument in England.

HENRY VIII *r.* 1509-47

AFTER THE PERVADING GLOOM OF Henry Tudor's last years, Henry VIII came to the throne on the crest of a wave of popularity, for this handsome, beardless youth of seventeen embodied a new age and seemed the antithesis of his father. He was tall and well proportioned, with a 'fine calf to his leg', had a fair complexion and auburn hair 'combed short and straight in the French fashion'; indeed, he was 'altogether the handsomest potentate I have ever set eyes on', wrote an envoy not given to exaggeration, and there was no hint that this young man with the figure and features of a Greek god would one day swell into a gross Goliath. He was athletic, riding well, accurate in his marksmanship in the butts and determined to shine in jousts; but if he had led a sheltered life and was quite unprepared for the tasks of kingship, he had none the less received an enviable general education, understanding Latin easily, speaking French fluently, a boy with a profound interest in theological questions and in the problems of scholarship which worried his friend Desiderus Erasmus, and possessing a flair for music-making of all kinds. He dressed superbly and by his natural grace commanded the stage with easy authority.

There was no question that here was a strong personality, who would leave an indelible mark on his country. 'Hitherto small mention has been made of King Henry', commented a Venetian in London, 'whereas for the future the whole world will talk of him', and that shrewd commentator Machiavelli (who never met him) described Henry by repute as 'rich, ferocious and greedy for glory'. Here was a Renaissance prince to his fingertips, who was determined to make his court a centre for the arts and humane studies. Unlike Henry VII the

Opposite: A portrait of Henry VIII from the school of Hans Holbein, showing the King as no longer the lithe, well-proportioned youth who succeeded to the throne in 1509.

new King showed himself to his people everywhere, for he knew that showmanship was a most necessary branch of statesmanship.

On his deathbed his father had advised him to marry Catherine of Aragon, the widow of his ill-fated elder brother Prince Arthur, to whom the young king had been betrothed since his twelfth birthday, to preserve the Spanish alliance. She was now twenty-three, petite beside Henry, but dainty and graceful, with fine eyes, and since he was young enough to be in love with love, he became captivated by the Princess it was his duty to wed. They were married at Greenwich six weeks after the accession, to enable the coronation in Westminster Abbey on Michaelmas Day to be a double crowning. There was prolonged merry-making at court in those early weeks. Henry had inherited a full Treasury and was open-handed; there were lavish banquets, masques, dances and tournaments. 'Our time is spent in continual festival', wrote the Queen. More mature than her husband, Catherine's sense of dignity corrected his flamboyance and added a note of seriousness without dampening his high spirits.

Henry had been content to leave the direction of affairs to Archbishop Warham, who was Lord Chancellor, Bishop Foxe and Surrey, the Lord Treasurer, though he had sacrificed his father's hated ministers Empson and Dudley to popular demand. The death of his grandmother, the remarkable Lady Margaret Beaufort, Countess of Richmond, a devout woman and a great patroness of learning, snapped a link with the past and before long Henry would be playing a more independent role, especially in foreign affairs. Since he was anxious to earn a reputation as a military commander no less than to back a right-eous cause, he joined the Holy League, formed by Pope Julius II with Venice and Spain against France, whose conquests in Italy had destroyed the balance of power. In 1513 he himself led an expedition across the Channel, resuming the Hundred Years' War. Even if he missed the battle of the Spurs, his presence at the sieges of Thérouanne and Tournai gave him a taste for campaigning he never lost; fighting an enemy was in quite a different category from jousting in Greenwich tiltyard, and even as an old man of 'chronic disease and great obesity' he insisted on taking the field again in 1544. While Henry was away in France, Surrey won a signal victory over the Scots at Flodden, leaving Henry's elder sister, Queen Margaret, Regent for the infant James V.

The preparations for the French campaign and the advantageous peace secured from Louis XII owed most to the King's almoner, Thomas Wolsey, who so impressed Henry by his ability that he was promoted

Opposite: Desiderius Erasmus the prominent Dutch humanist and friend of Henry VIII. While in Cambridge during the years 1511–14, Erasmus produced his Greek edition of the New Testament.

Archbishop of York in 1514, a year later was appointed a cardinal and soon afterwards succeeded Warham as Lord Chancellor. From 1515 to the summer of 1529 Wolsey's rule was undisputed. He had won the King's confidence and Henry delegated more and more to him, while he followed his own bent in field-sports and music. From time to time he would bestir himself to take greater interest in diplomacy and administration, yet for all his talents he was lazy, found paperwork distasteful and lacked powers of concentration, so that increasingly the partnership with the Cardinal became one-sided. Wolsey was the last English ecclesiastic to rule in the medieval tradition, and perhaps the greatest. He amassed benefices, holding in succession the richest bishoprics in addition to his archbishopric, and he was also Abbot of England's wealthiest religious house, St Alban's Abbey. With these enormous revenues he indulged in his passion for building at York Place in Whitehall and at Hampton Court, of which Henry grew envious, and lived in great pomp. Though granted special powers as a papal legate, the Cardinal took little interest in Church reform; he stood for the status quo and

Portrait of Thomas Wolsey, Cardinal of York and Lord Chancellor. Wolsey was Henry's favourite and effectively wielded power from 1515 until his fall from grace in 1529.

seriously underestimated people's dissatisfaction with clerical control, and while he was a skilled diplomatist he neglected domestic affairs. Men talked of him as if he were more powerful than the King himself, yet he was entirely dependent on Henry's favour and when he lost it he was finished.

Under the peace treaty with France in 1514 Henry's younger sister Mary, 'a nymph from heaven' of seventeen, was married off to the aged King Louis XII, still anxious to be father to a son, but he died soon afterwards and Mary impetuously made a runaway match with Charles Brandon, Duke of Suffolk, a boon companion of Henry's. They were pardoned, on being required to pay a crippling fine, and after long exile in the country Suffolk returned to court to become Wolsey's severest critic. From this marriage sprang the Suffolk line to the succession, for their elder daughter Frances married Henry Grey, to give birth to Lady Jane Grey and her sisters.

Mid-eighteenth-century engraving of Mary, Queen of France and Charles Brandon, Duke of Suffolk. Mary, a 'nymph from heaven', married Louis XII of France in 1514; after his death she eloped with Suffolk, who, upon his return to Henry VIII's court, became a severe critic of Wolsey.

The old Europe was changing, and changing much faster than England. The rapid expansion of Spain's empire in the New World and Portugal's exploitation of the Eastern spice trade were to revolutionise the economies of the European nations. With these discoveries Europe was ceasing to be a Mediterranean continent, for there was a shift of balance to north-west Europe. Humanism, which embraced a fearless search for truth and beauty, questioned the purpose of man, and the search led inevitably to dispute with the authority of the Church. Yet England remained surprisingly orthodox. The contacts of John Colet and other scholars with Italy had made them anxious to reform the Church from within, much as Erasmus desired, but in England, if pockets of Lollardry remained and anticlericalism increased under Wolsey, there was no incident approaching the issue

ASSERTIO SEPTEM SA=
cramentorum aduersus Martin.
Lutherū,ædita ab inuictis=
simo Angliæ et Fran=
ciæ rege, et do.Hy=
berniæ Henri=
co eius no
minis
o=
ctauo.

The title page of Henry's
1521 pamphlet *Assertio
Septem Sacramentorum Adversus
Martinum Lutherum*. In this
work Henry supported the
papacy and attacked the ideas
of Martin Luther. For his
condemnation of Luther,
Henry was granted the title
'Defender of the Faith' by
Pope Clement VII.

of Luther's theses at Wittenburg, which launched a specifically Protestant Reformation. England was regarded by popes as a most loyal member-state of Christendom and her King an apostle of orthodoxy. Indeed Henry felt it his mission to write a tract against Luther, the *Defence of the Seven Sacraments*, and though Thomas More and John Fisher helped him, the book was turned by his pen in 1521 into a most effective essay in Catholic polemics. In later life he regretted some of his statements here about the indissolubility of marriage and about papal power: 'What serpent so venomously crept in as he who calls the most Holy See of Rome "Babylon" and the Pope's authority "Tyrannical"?' Dedicated to Leo X, that all might see Henry 'was ready to defend the church not only with his armies, but with the resources of his mind', the book caused a great stir and became a best-seller on the continent; not until Queen Victoria's *Leaves from the Journal of Our Life in the Highlands* would an English royal author be so successful.

In recognition of his championship of the church Henry was given the title *Fidei Defensor*, which was confirmed by the golden bull of 1524, and though this did not make the title hereditary, its use by subsequent kings and queens of England was to be warranted by an Act of Parliament in 1544.

In France the dashing Francis I had replaced Louis XII, while in Spain Charles of Ghent had succeeded the foxy Ferdinand. The Emperor Maximilian, who had transformed the Habsburg monarchy and strengthened its hold on the Netherlands, was approaching his end. He had recently contemplated resigning the headship of the Holy Roman Empire to Henry VIII and when Maximilian died in January 1519, Henry, no less than Francis, decided to stand for election, for he was captivated by the mystique of the Empire and wanted to be recognised as the leader of Christendom; he was the most experienced of the contestants, and the senior, being six years older than Francis and nine older than Charles. But the seven imperial electors wanted only a Habsburg to rule the confederation of German states and Charles V became the victor. Personal rivalry between the three sovereigns, each of whom regarded himself as the embodiment of Renaissance chivalry, dominated European politics for another thirty years. Habsburg–Valois disputes in Italy, Flanders and the Rhine Valley made each turn to England for support, and despite Wolsey's aim to preserve neutrality as a method of holding the balance of power, Henry found it hard to overcome his own animosity towards Francis I and his inherited conviction that France was the traditional enemy.

Wolsey's finest hour was the glittering gathering of the Field of Cloth of Gold which he devised for Henry to meet Francis, near

Francis I, King of France, *c.* 1540. Francis succeeded Louis XII on 1 January 1515.

Fresco depicting the entry
of Francis I of France and
Charles V of Spain into Paris.
After the death of the Holy
Roman Emperor Maximilian
in 1519, Henry VIII, Francis I
and Charles V competed to
become the new leader of
Christendom. Charles was the
eventual victor.

Henry VIII embarking from Dover, 31 May 1520, for the 'Field of Cloth of Gold' summit meeting with Francis I. It dominated the summer of 1520 but failed to bury old animosities.

Guisnes. This was intended as a summit meeting to guarantee the peace of Europe. The two Kings were supported by the greatest in their realms who spent four weeks from midsummer 1520 in banquets, jousts and other contests to celebrate the rebirth of chivalry, but the burial of old animosities never succeeded. Before and after the Field of Cloth of Gold, Henry had meetings with Charles v at Dover and then at Gravelines, but there was no duplicity on his part. Under Wolsey's guidance he hoped to extend the entente to the Empire, but Valois–Habsburg rivalry proved too strong.

Another opportunity for Henry to become 'arbiter of Europe' came with Pope Leo x's death, and he was anxious that Wolsey should be elected, for only once before had there been an English pope – Nicholas Brakespeare in the twelfth century. Despite much diplomatic activity and fair promises from both Charles and Francis, he failed and the Emperor's tutor, Adrian of Utrecht, became Pope. His pontificate was brief and Henry again pushed forward Wolsey's candidature with no better success.

Dynastic problems soon became enmeshed in the trammels of international politics. Henry had been overjoyed on New Year's Day 1511 when Catherine had presented him with a son, but the Prince Henry survived for no more than six weeks to their intense grief. Thereafter there was an unhappy series of miscarriages and still-births, but in 1516

the Queen gave birth to the Princess Mary, who seemed a healthy
enough infant. 'The Queen and I are both young', Henry told the
Venetian ambassador, 'and if it is a girl this time, by God's grace boys will
follow.' Alas, the Almighty withheld his blessing and with the passing of
the years it became painfully clear that no further children would be
born to Catherine. Until marriage Henry had been shy with women,
but Catherine had given him confidence and now he cast a roving eye
at the beauties at court. In 1519 his mistress Bessie Blount, who 'excelled
all other damsels in singing, dancing and goodly practices', gave him a
son, Henry Fitzroy, who was subsequently created Duke of Richmond
and groomed for the succession, but a natural son was a poor substitute
for a prince born in the purple. The Duke died in 1536, after marrying
the Duke of Norfolk's daughter.

Henry began to think that his marriage to Catherine was unfruit-
ful because it was against God's law, despite ample papal dispensations,

A copy of part of the letter
Catherine of Aragon wrote
to Henry on learning that
he was going to divorce her.

for he had disobeyed Holy Writ by marrying his deceased brother's wife and the more he dwelt on the matter the clearer it seemed to him that under canon law he was a bachelor who had been living in sin. No word of consolation, not even from the Pope himself, would satisfy him; Catherine was not, had never been, his lawful wife. He desperately wanted a son born in wedlock who could ultimately succeed to his throne unchallenged. Dynastic need and the burden on his conscience had become unsupportable by the beginning of 1527 and he prayed for the Church to give him the relief which was his due, requiring Wolsey to use his influence with Rome to declare unequivocally that his marriage with Catherine had been invalid so that he could marry again. Dissatisfaction with Catherine as a wife preceded his infatuation with Anne Boleyn, who was not content like her elder sister Mary to be a royal mistress, but wanted to be a queen consort, while Henry wanted a legitimate heir. Thus developed the 'King's Great Matter'.

Anne, the younger daughter of Sir Thomas Boleyn and Lady Elizabeth Howard, had been brought up in France in the household of Queen Claude and perhaps Henry first set eyes on both Boleyn girls at the Field of Cloth of Gold, when Anne was thirteen. She did not develop as a dazzling beauty, as Bessie Blount had been, yet she came to exercise an unprecedented fascination over the King. Her strongest points were her almond-shaped eyes and her raven hair, but she also possessed remarkable vivacity and acquired in France a flair for fashion which made Catherine seem downright dowdy. Her enemies remarked on the rudimentary sixth finger on her left hand – a sure sign, they said, of a sorceress. Before Henry had tired of her sister Mary, four years her senior, Anne had charmed Sir Thomas Wyatt, the poet, who lived near her parents' home of Hever Castle; and then came a more serious suitor, Sir Henry Percy, Northumberland's son, who was a ward of Wolsey's, but the Cardinal, sensing the King's interest in her, asked the Earl of Northumberland to call home his son. Sensual love letters survive from 1527 in which Henry assures Anne of his undying devotion: 'I would you were in mine arms or I in yours for I think it is a long time since we kissed.' He somehow saw himself as a chivalrous knight, protecting that same 'virtue' which she so vigorously defended. It was marriage or nothing. In February 1528 he told her that with the negotiations Wolsey had in hand 'shortly you and I shall have our desired end'. Neither foresaw the difficulties ahead in his achieving a separation from Catherine, but each setback over the

Opposite: A seventeenth-century portrait of Anne Boleyn, by Frans Pourbus the younger, which shows off her best features – her eyes and her jet-black hair. Her marriage to Henry VIII lasted only three years, during which time she bore the future Elizabeth I and miscarried the male heir Henry so fervently wanted.

Gold half sovereign struck
during the reign of Henry VIII.

next five years made him long more fervently for Anne as his true wife.

The sack of Rome by imperialist troops in 1527 made Pope Clement VII a puppet of Charles V, who would never consent to his aunt Catherine being cast aside, and despite great activity Wolsey failed to secure a satisfactory verdict from Rome. The most Clement would do was to issue a commission jointly to Cardinals Campeggio and Wolsey to hold a court in London which could hear the parties but make no judgement. Queen Catherine for her part refused to acknowledge the authority of the court, but in a moving speech appealed to her husband: 'This twenty years I have been your true wife … And when ye had me at the first I take God to be my judge, I was a true maid without taint of man.' At the end of the law-term Campeggio adjourned the court, to procrastinate further before the suit was removed to Rome, and this signalled Wolsey's fall. Parliament was summoned for the autumn, when the cry was 'Down with the Church', and after a period of ineffectual shadow-boxing with the papacy, Henry hearkened to the advice of Thomas Cromwell that England must break away from papal allegiance as the necessary preliminary for him to be legally rid of his wife. Wolsey was spared an attainder and allowed to retain his archbishopric. He had never visited his province and on the eve of his enthronement in York Minster in November 1530 he was arrested on suspicion of treason, but died on his journey south to face his accusers. As Cardinal Legate and Lord Chancellor he had combined the reins of government in both Church and State and now, under Cromwell's astute guidance, the Reformation Parliament made Henry Pope, as well as King, in his own dominions. He became Supreme Head of the Church of England, a national Church which retained its medieval organisation but lacked a firm confession of faith.

Henry secretly married Anne in January 1533 and, following Archbishop Cranmer's judgement at Dunstable that Henry's marriage to Catherine had been null and void since its beginning, she was crowned Queen in Westminster Abbey at Whitsun, the folds of her robes concealing her pregnancy. She was imperious and unpopular, for there was great sympathy for Catherine of Aragon, who now reverted to her former title of Princess of Wales and lived out her remaining days at Ampthill and Kimbolton manors with a tiny household, whose wages were always in arrears. She was heartbroken, but remained firm in her Catholic faith and died in January 1536. Henry celebrated her death by dressing from head to foot in yellow.

The King had confiscated the Cardinal's residences and made extensive alterations to them. York Place, with which Anne was enchanted, was transformed into Whitehall Palace and it soon covered twenty-four acres, the largest palace in the Western world, symbolising, no less effectively than Holbein's portraits, the power of the new monarchy. At the same time he took over the neighbouring site of the Hospital of St James, where he built St James's Palace; the royal initials 'H.S.' are still depicted in the brickwork of the Clock Tower. Before long, out of the spoils of the monasteries, Henry embarked on the Palace of Nonsuch in Surrey, a fantastic pleasure dome, with its strange turrets and pinnacles and the intricate carving and plasterwork of the inner court dominated by a massive statue of the King.

It was Greenwich which Anne had chosen for her lying-in and here she gave birth in September 1533 to Princess Elizabeth. Henry treated mother and child coldly; it was not for another daughter that he had broken with Rome and made Anne his Queen, but the child was healthy and precocious and he hoped a son would follow. To distract himself he took immense personal interest in the legislation Cromwell was devising to make him supreme in his own domain and to make government more efficient; there was brought about an administrative revolution to modernise the workings of the old medieval departments of state even while the Reformation Parliament was still in session. The King was adamant that his decisions over Anne and the Church, ratified by Parliament, should be unreservedly supported by all his subjects, through the taking of an oath to the succession. Sir Thomas More, who had been close to Henry and had succeeded Wolsey as Lord Chancellor, would only swear if the oath could be so framed that it did not imply his own sanction to the repudiation of the Pope's authority or the invalidity of Henry's first marriage. Neither More nor Bishop Fisher of Rochester, the two men whose support Henry wanted most, would go against their conscience; they were tried for treason and executed, yet the King feared their stand on principle would be interpreted abroad as a powerful witness against his rule.

The family of Sir Thomas More, from a miniature by Rowland Lockey. Despite his position as Henry VIII's Lord Chancellor, Sir Thomas would not go against his conscience in swearing an oath to the Succession. For his challenge to Henry's wishes he was tried for treason and executed.

F. Maria fil Ioh Scroope, Ar. frat. Henrici Dñi Scroope,
G. Dno filij dictor Tho Mor. et Mar. Vx. eius.
H. Tres filiæ Tho. Mori Dñi Cancellary Anglice.

In the same month in which Catherine died, Henry had a serious accident while riding in the lists and his life seemed in danger. Norfolk brought the news to his royal niece and, according to her, the shock was so great that it brought on the miscarriage of a male child. Henry was so angered that nothing could save her; he talked about being 'seduced by witchcraft' when he married her, and others said the Queen must have a defective constitution. Already Jane Seymour was waiting in the wings. There was enough circumstantial evidence that Anne had behaved indiscreetly and in the highly-charged atmosphere at court, chivalrous attention could be transformed by a gesture into passionate devotion. First Mark Smeaton, a lutanist, confessed on the rack to adultery with the Queen; then Henry Norris was implicated, two other Gentlemen of the Chamber and finally her own brother, Lord Rochford. Henry was convinced of the guilt of all five men and his own profligacy assured him that Anne's own behaviour had been utterly libidinous – an English Messalina. She was tried after her alleged lovers had all been found guilty and was executed on Tower Green on 19 May 1536. The same day Cranmer issued a dispensation allowing Henry to marry Jane Seymour.

Jane was the daughter of Sir John Seymour, a Wiltshire knight who had served with Henry in France in 1513, while her mother, a Wentworth, was descended from Edward III. She was now twenty-five, fair, of medium height, rather pale-faced, and with a reputation for modesty and an inclination towards the Reformed faith. She was married to Henry in the Queen's Chapel, Whitehall, on 30 May, but her coronation, arranged for the autumn, never took place because of the plague. She chose as her motto 'Bound to obey and serve' and realised her essential role was as mother of England's heir, but first she acted as peacemaker between Henry and Princess Mary. On Trinity Sunday 1537 a *Te Deum* was sung 'for joy of the Queen's quickening of child' – an unprecedented step in the development of the liturgy – and on 12 October in Hampton Court she bore a son in a difficult confinement which cost her her own life. In dynastic terms Jane had achieved all that had been expected of her and, alone of Henry's Queens, she was buried in St George's Chapel, Windsor. When ten years later he was called to his maker he ordered that his coffin should be laid beside hers, for Jane had given him, after twenty-eight years of ruling, the Prince he had wanted, Edward, Prince of Wales.

Cromwell had enriched Henry beyond his wildest imaginings through dissolving first the smaller religious houses and then the

Opposite: Jane Seymour, the third wife of Henry VIII. Although married to Henry for little over a year she provided him with the heir he desperately wanted. Edward, Prince of Wales, was born on 12 October 1537; twelve days later, having failed to recover from a difficult labour, Jane Seymour died.

greater monasteries, provoking the one serious threat of the entire reign, the Pilgrimage of Grace. The insurgents were suppressed as ruthlessly as the abbots who refused to surrender their houses. At the same time an authoritative English Bible based on the work of Coverdale and Tyndale was required to be placed in all churches and Cromwell and Cranmer began doctrinal discussions with the German Lutherans. Isolated in Europe Henry cast about for an ally, for when Francis I and Charles V signed a ten-year truce Henry feared they would join forces to invade England to put into practice the papal bull deposing him. This search for an alliance with Protestant states became caught up in Henry's search for a further wife and as a result he married Anne of Cleves, whose portrait by Holbein had been so flattering, in January 1540. Fearful of the consequences of the Cleves alliance if he were not to proceed with the marriage he went through with the ceremony, but found his bride from the Rhenish principality impossible; she spoke no English, had no accomplishments and, worst of all, was the antithesis of beauty. Their marriage was never consummated and once more he turned to Cromwell, the minister who had arranged the match, to secure a divorce.

While the Cleves marriage negotiation had been in progress, a Catholic reaction had begun in England, through the initiative of Stephen Gardiner, Bishop of Winchester, and Treasurer Norfolk. They had the King's ear and Henry himself came down to the Lords for the debate on the Act of Six Articles; persecutions of Anabaptists followed, though Cromwell endeavoured to mitigate the operation of the law. Henry had barely created him Earl of Essex, when he was arrested at the Council table as a result of a well-planned conspiracy of Norfolk and Gardiner. He had not attempted to procure a royal divorce because he knew that once free from Anne of Cleves Henry would marry the beautiful and orthodox Catherine Howard, niece of his enemy Norfolk. He was condemned for treasonable heresy and for the moment even the King believed he was a sacramentary and had been too close to the Lutherans. With the Habsburg-Valois struggle renewed his policy was out-dated.

Norfolk might have profited from Cromwell's fall had the young Catherine Howard not proved such a liability. She had, like Anne Boleyn, been schooled for court and the royal bed but then it came out that she continued adulterous relations with Francis Dereham, an old flame, and with Thomas Culpeper. Henry vowed he would cut off her

head with his own sword, and then self-pity overcame rage and he 'regretted his ill luck in meeting with such ill-conditioned wives'. She was executed on 13 February 1542.

After such experiences few imagined Henry would embark on a sixth marriage, yet the next year he married Catherine Parr, who had already buried two husbands, Sir Edward Burrough and Lord Latymer. She was a blue-stocking of thirty-three, who though childless had successfully brought up three step-children. She was amazed at Henry's proposal, but loyally responded it was 'the greatest joy and comfort' to look after him and his children. By now lonely, and much troubled by his ulcerous leg, which had developed from his fall in 1536, Henry wanted an intellectual companion who could make a home for his family. She succeeded in meeting his expectations as nurse and step-mother, though he disapproved of her friendship with the Cambridge Reformers. Edward, Mary and Elizabeth were all brought to court and she took the closest interest in their education. Catherine also encouraged Henry's foundation of Trinity College, Cambridge, and his transformation of the rump of Wolsey's Cardinal College, Oxford, into Christ Church.

In those last few years of the reign Gardiner fought for Catholic dogma, while Henry supported Cranmer in a much more broadly-based church. At the political level there was a struggle for the regency when Edward should succeed, in which the main contestants were Norfolk and the Prince's uncle Edward Seymour, Earl of Hertford. It was Hertford who won the final laurels of the French war, while Norfolk was compromised by his son Surrey's treason. Here, as in the doctrinal dispute, Henry aimed at a consensus. By his will no single minister would direct affairs after he had gone, but a balanced Council of Regents. The Colossus who had founded the modern English nation state died in the early hours of 28 January 1547 in Whitehall, with Thomas Cranmer at his side, but his wife and children were deliberately kept away. He wanted no farewells.

Opposite: Anne of Cleves, Queen of England. Henry married Anne, his fourth wife, in January 1540, in the hope of gaining alliances with Protestant states. Henry was not impressed by his bride and did not consummate the marriage.

EDWARD VI *r.* 1547-53

'GOD'S IMP', HENRY VIII'S SON by his third wife, Jane Seymour, was born at Hampton Court on 12 October 1537 as a result of a Caesarean section. As Bishop Latimer remarked, 'We all hungered after a prince so long that there was as much rejoicing as at the birth of John the Baptist.' His mother never recovered from the ordeal of childbirth, but died 'through the fault of them that were about her, who suffered her to take great cold and to eat things that her fantasy in sickness called for'. Yet the fact that the boy had lived and seemed healthy enough quite put his mother's death in the shade.

Elaborate precautions were taken to safeguard Prince Edward's health to protect him from the slightest risk of infection and no less elaborate rules were drawn up for his education and his spiritual development, so that in the fullness of time he would be fully prepared to succeed his father as King and Supreme Head of the Church of England. In March 1538 the Prince was assigned a separate establishment at Hunsdon in Hertfordshire in which the key figure was Lady Bryan, a woman of long experience of royal nurseries. His father remained torn between having Edward at court to lavish affection on him and show him off as a proud parent who, after twenty-eight years as King, had at last solved the intractable problem of the succession, or leaving the child safely at a manor house in country air. The motherless boy's relations with his father before Henry's final marriage to Catherine Parr were non-existent; as he later wrote in his personal chronicle, until he was six years he was 'brought up among the women' – including his half-sisters Elizabeth, four years his senior, and for some of the time, Mary, a grown woman of twenty-one. Catherine Parr, however, felt it would be in the

Opposite: Edward, Prince of Wales: the male heir born to Henry VIII after twenty-eight years of frustration.

PARVVLE PATRISSA, PATRIÆ VIRTVTIS ET HÆRES
  ESTO, NIHIL MAIVS MAXIMVS ORBIS HABET.
GNATVM VIX POSSVNT COELVM ET NATVRA DEDISSE,
  HVIVS QVEM PATRIS, VICTVS HONORET HONOS.
ÆQVATO TANTVM, TANTI TV FACTA PARENTIS.
  VOTA HOMINVM, VIX QVO PROGREDIANTVR, HABENT
VINCITO, VICISTI, QVOT REGES PRISCVS ADORAT
  ORBIS, NEC TE QVI VINCERE POSSIT, ERIT

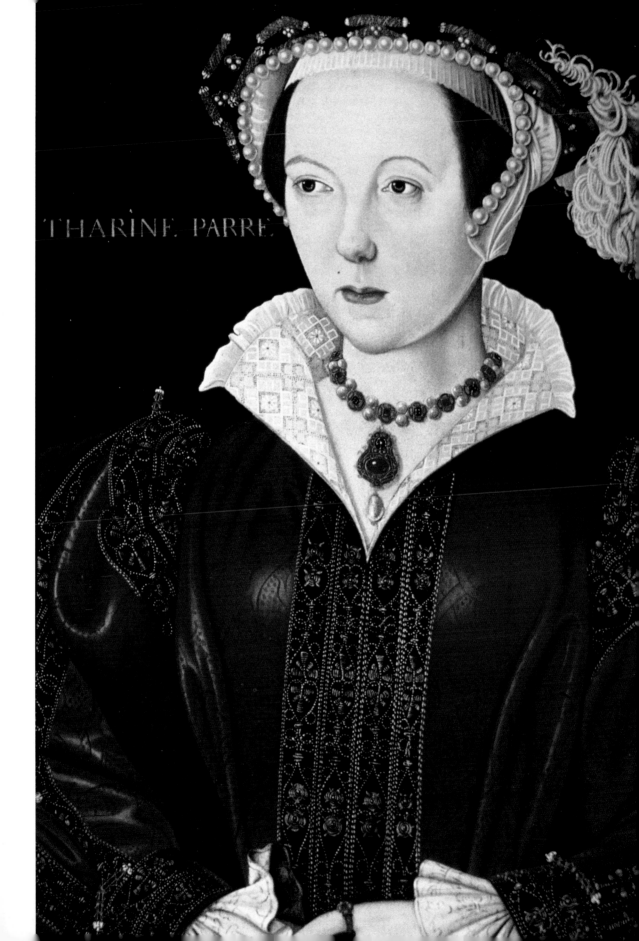

THARINE. PARRE

Prince's best interests to spend longer periods at court, since his whole education was being framed to help him in his future responsibilities. At last she had her way and this extraordinary family became reunited.

On Catherine Parr's recommendation Richard Cox, a Cambridge humanist, was given formal charge of Edward's studies while John Cheke, professor of Greek in the same university, was appointed his regular tutor. Cox told King Henry that his six-year-old charge 'undertaketh and can frame pretty Latins … and is now ready to enter into some proper and profitable fables of Aesop and other wholesome and godly lessons'. Cox and Cheke were both scholars in the Erasmian tradition – humanists concerned with learning, not ministers preaching a gospel – and neither would have dared to indoctrinate the Prince with the advanced views of some of the Cambridge Reformers during the years of Catholic reaction which came with Cromwell's fall. Little Edward heard Mass daily, for 'every day in the mass time he readeth a portion of Solomon's proverbs', learning from them 'to fear God's commandments, to beware of strange and wanton women, to be obedient to father and mother and to be thankful to him that telleth him of his faults'. The precocious child was schooled in conscientious duty, 'in part to satisfy the good expectations of the King's Majesty' – as he himself put it; in part because he could never hope to be wholly satisfactory to his father, nor to God, and the Almighty must have seemed to him as a heavenly version of his earthly father.

His was an unbending curriculum which, as he described it himself, included 'learning of tongues, of the Scriptures, of philosophy and the liberal sciences'. Perhaps it is fitting that Edward's name is chiefly remembered today as the nominal founder of a score of grammar schools, such as Birmingham and Southampton, when a small proportion of chantry and other ecclesiastical revenues were diverted to educational purposes during his reign. If he appears as rather a prig, it is worth remembering that on occasion Dr Cox beat him for failing in his lessons and also that the life of the schoolroom was leavened by riding, archery and music-making.

Nor was Edward alone, for Catherine brought in boys of much the same age to share his lessons and sports, including Henry Brandon, Duke of Suffolk, Lord Thomas Howard and Barnaby Fitzpatrick, son of an Irish peer, who was Edward's closest friend, and one girl, Jane Dormer, with whom he would dance.

Edward was not yet ten years old when his father died on 28 January

Opposite: Portrait of Catherine Parr, the sixth wife of Henry VIII; she had a great effect on the King's relationship with his son.

The coronation procession of Edward VI ran from the Tower of London along East Cheap, past Bow Church into Cheapside, past the spire of old St Paul's and down the Strand to Westminster.

1547, leaving as he believed careful constitutional arrangements for the government of the realm during his minority. However, the new King's uncle, Edward Seymour, Earl of Hertford, seized power, overturning the Council of Regents to establish himself as Protector of the realm and sole guardian of the boy King, who soon created him Duke of Somerset. Edward became puppet of a faction for under Somerset's rule England

became established unequivocally as a Protestant state. The Catholic Act of Six Articles of 1539 was repealed, the chantries were abolished and an English Prayer Book was issued in 1549, which owed most to the genius of Thomas Cranmer. This new Reformation was enforced by an Act of Uniformity for public worship and it was to take an even more radical turn with the preparation of a Second Prayer Book in 1552, in which the central doctrine of the service of Holy Communion was declared to be no more than a commemorative rite. Gone were the veneration of saints and remembrance of the departed; in churches there was widespread iconoclasm, for monuments were defaced, wall-paintings covered with whitewash and stained-glass windows removed if they betrayed any hint of medieval superstition. The Bible was enthroned and the glosses of the early Fathers of the Church cast down. Henry VIII's attempt to pursue a middle course had been abandoned with a

Thomas Cranmer, Archbishop of Canterbury to Henry VIII, Edward VI and Mary I, who perished at the stake in the fires at Smithfield.

vengeance, and King Edward's tutors and chaplains so influenced his development that despite his tender years he was in the vanguard of the movement for Protestant truth.

Anti-Papal cartoon depicting Bishops Latimar and Ridley and Archbishop Cranmer.

It is a bizarre thought that Somerset sought to enforce the 1543 treaty with Scotland under which Edward was to have been betrothed to the infant Mary Queen of Scots, for these Tudor and 'Stuart' royal offspring were poles apart in their beliefs and general attitudes. Somerset defeated the Scots army at Pinkie near Musselburgh and then captured Edinburgh, but the Catholic Mary was sent into France to be educated as a French princess and was betrothed to the Dauphin. The Protector explored the possibility of a union of England and Scotland without success.

The summer of 1549 saw two serious threats to the regime, the rising in the west country in protest at the English Prayer Book, which was suppressed by Lord Russell, and Kett's Rebellion in Norfolk, largely a movement against the enclosure of common fields, where the insurgents were routed by John Dudley, Earl of Warwick, son of Henry VII's finance minister. Warwick exploited his success by challenging the autocratic rule of Protector Somerset, who was outmanoeuvred, sent to the Tower and subsequently executed. Although the Duke of Northumberland (as

Warwick became in 1551) never took the title of Protector, he concentrated offices and power in his hands and was ambitious for his family.

Edward VI had been kept busy at his studies. By 1550 the 'Royal Imp' had read the *Ethics* of Aristotle in the original Greek and was translating Cicero's *De Philosophia* from Latin into Greek. Even more so than the great seal of England, the boy King was *clavis regni*: 'the Key to the Kingdom'. To establish control over his person was to become the effective ruler. Sir Thomas Seymour, the Lord Admiral and Somerset's younger brother, had married the Queen Dowager, Catherine Parr, and tried to bribe Edward with pocket money. Now Northumberland sought to persuade him to use his undoubted power and rule as his father had, sure that Edward would not go against his wishes. Princess Elizabeth sewed shirts for her half-brother and wrote him touching little letters in Latin, yet Mary stayed aloof from court, very conscious of the pitfalls. Edward did not return their affection and showed no emotion when his uncles, the Protector and Admiral Seymour, were executed, nor when his step-mother, Queen Catherine, died in childbed.

The King became fanatically Protestant, as his mentors had intended, yet the future of Protestantism in England hung on the slender thread of the sickly boy's life. If he died without issue the Crown would pass to his elder sister, Mary, the child of Catherine of Aragon, who was no less fanatically Catholic in her beliefs. By mid-1552 there was no doubt about the King's frailty and even courtiers regarded him as a living corpse. Northumberland was led to make his desperate gamble to alter the succession in favour of Lady Jane Grey, the eldest daughter of Henry Grey, Marquess of Suffolk, by Frances Brandon, who was the daughter of Mary, younger sister of Henry VIII. Northumberland hurriedly married his son Guildford Dudley to Lady Jane and easily obtained King Edward's signature to the document to alter the succession in her favour, which was witnessed by twenty-six peers. Recent research suggests that in this Edward was not the innocent dupe of Northumberland's scheming, but was himself most anxious to preserve the Protestant succession. The salvation of England was for him more important than the doctrine of legitimacy embodied in his half-sister Mary. The consumptive, delirious youth died at Greenwich on 6 July 1553 in his sixteenth year, assured that as he had done his duty, the gates of Hell would not prevail, while good Bishop Ridley told crowds at St Paul's Cross that Jane must be acknowledged as the rightful Queen.

Opposite: Henry's delicate and short-lived heir Edward VI, painted in the manner of William Scrots.

MARY I *r. 1553-8*

HE ONE SURVIVING CHILD OF Henry VIII by Catherine of Aragon, Mary, was born at Greenwich Palace on 18 February 1516 and there was much rejoicing that the baby lived, even though she was a girl. She was christened at the Friary Church, outside the palace gates, where her parents had been married, and her godparents were Cardinal Wolsey and the Duchess of Norfolk, wife of the victor of Flodden. From her birth King Henry looked on his daughter as a useful pawn in the great game of dynastic diplomacy and in 1518 the first of a long series of proxy marriages for her took place when she was formally betrothed to the Dauphin of France. When Wolsey lifted the little girl in his arms to place a tiny ring on her finger, leaving it to the French Admiral Bonnivet to 'pass it over the second joint', Mary said to the Admiral, 'Are you the Dauphin? If you are, I want to kiss you.' Alas, Mary was destined to take part in several abortive betrothals to foreign princes and by the time she was twenty-eight feared she would always remain a spinster, for she had longed for a husband and children of her own. When suitors came, she said, 'there was nothing to be got but fine words and while my father lives I shall be only the Lady Mary, the most unhappy lady in Christendom'.

Mary was to remain devoted to her mother's memory, yet the later parallels drawn between Catherine of Aragon and her daughter have tended to obscure the characteristics which the Princess inherited from her father. She had the same precociousness as all Henry's children and he was proud of her. She could play the virginals when she was four and soon began a most strict regimen of study on plans drawn up by Vives, the Spanish philosopher, so that she was sent from court under the care

Opposite: Mary I, Queen of England. Catholic, half-Spanish and eventually married to Philip of Spain, Mary was torn between two interests and never understood her native people.

Mary laying on hands to cure the 'queen's evil', the name given to scrofula (or 'king's evil') for the supposed power of monarchs to heal it.

first of the Countess of Salisbury and then of Lady Shelton, following the philosopher's precept that 'cherishing marreth sons, but utterly destroyeth daughters'. She was by nature stubborn and strong-willed and, as she developed, failed to regard compromise as anything but a betrayal of weakness.

Once the rift between Henry and Catherine developed, Mary was sent to Ludlow as Princess of Wales (as Arthur had been by Henry VII, though for very different reasons) and was agonisingly deprived of her mother's company. Inevitably she took her mother's side in the King's Great Matter, and Anne Boleyn hated her for it. Once Anne, as Queen, had produced a rival princess, she demanded that Mary's ears be boxed 'for the cursed bastard she is' and at Hatfield the seventeen-year-old girl was now assigned the pokiest room in the house, deprived of her personal maids and made to serve as lady-in-waiting to her baby half-sister. The animosity between Catherine and Anne was understandably to be continued in the next generation by their respective daughters. Mary was heartbroken at her mother's death. In her last hours Catherine had written to Henry, pleading with him to be a good father to Mary and to preserve her rights to the succession.

With Anne Boleyn's fall, there was a chance of *rapprochement*, for Jane Seymour desperately wanted to reconcile Henry with Mary. She was now twenty, with a mind of her own, and persistently refused to recognise her father as Supreme Head of the Church, for this contradicted all she had learned about religion from her earliest years. The Duke of Norfolk told her if she had been *his* daughter he would have knocked her head 'against the wall until it was as soft as baked apple'. At last Cromwell, with the help of Chapuys, the imperial ambassador, succeeded in bringing home to Mary the peril in which she lay. He sent her a draft letter in grovelling terms which he told her to copy out verbatim and sign, making her submission to Henry. This she did, making mental reservations about the Pope's authority, and when summoned to court to acknowledge her faults personally before her father, 'most humbly laying at his feet', the worst of their estrangement was over.

Above all Mary wanted to be taken back within his family circle: 'I would rather be a chamberer, having the fruitions of Your Highness' presence than an empress away from it.' Henry was overjoyed that his 'chiefest jewel' was again living with him, though Mary was still under the slur of bastardy. Prince Edward's birth brought the two sisters together, for both must now give way to a brother; yet there were seventeen years between them. At Hunsdon Mary taught Elizabeth to play cards for stakes and encouraged her fool to amuse her with his antics.

King Henry's final marriage meant much to Mary, for she was now more regularly at court than at any time since 1530 and she regarded Queen Catherine Parr as more of a sister than yet another step-mother. Catherine showed her many kindnesses and for the first time the Princess had an adequate allowance for clothes. The Queen suggested Mary should undertake a translation of Erasmus's paraphrases of the New Testament, which she began and Nicholas Udall completed when her ill-health made serious study impossible. Mary suffered much illness throughout the 1540s.

On Edward VI's succession the Protector's brother Admiral Seymour attempted to make a bid for Mary's hand before turning his attentions to the Queen Dowager, when he implored the Princess to use her influence with Catherine Parr to accept him. Mary wisely refrained – 'I being a maid am nothing cunning' in love affairs. Such circumspection did not desert her throughout the reign, when the revolution in religion was anathema to her. No one, not even her royal half-brother, knew how they might 'turn her opinions'. She resided quietly, outside London, waiting for sickly Edward's demise, but praying for him fervently. When Northumberland had Lady Jane Grey proclaimed Queen in London, Mary was in Suffolk and the country rallied to her, content to allow the succession to take its proper course, even if the sovereign were a woman, single and at heart a Catholic.

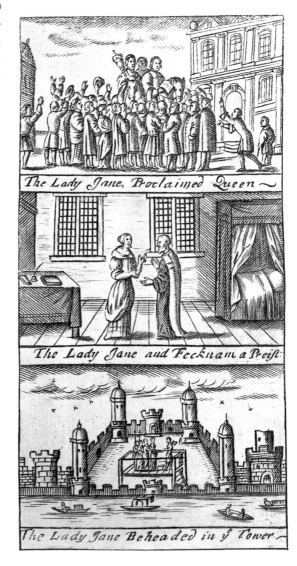

Cartoon depicting the events of the nine-day rule of Lady Jane Grey. After her succession, the country rallied to support Mary as the natural successor to the throne and Jane Grey was beheaded.

The Lady Jane, Proclaimed Queen

The Lady Jane and Fecknam a Preist

The Lady Jane Beheaded in y Tower

The two faces of the medal struck to commemorate the marriage of Mary Tudor and Philip of Spain in 1554.

Opposite: A portrait of Cardinal Reginald Pole, Mary's leading minister, who became deeply unpopular for his part in the burnings of the martyrs. He was later to reconcile England with the Church of Rome.

The question was whom should Mary, the first Queen Regnant since Matilda challenged Stephen's accession in 1135, marry? She sought the advice of Simon Renard, Charles v's ambassador, telling him she had 'never felt that which is called love, nor harboured thoughts of voluptuousness'. His list of eight possible bridegrooms was reduced to a single name, Philip II of Spain, a widower, and reports of his religious orthodoxy delighted her no less than his portrait. In her private oratory, accompanied by Renard and a lady-in-waiting, Mary led the saying of the *Veni Creator* and solemnly declared she would marry Philip and 'love him perfectly'. A marriage treaty was signed in November. By then Parliament had begun to dismantle the Edwardian Reformation settlement and the Roman Mass was again celebrated. In due course Cardinal Reginald Pole would return to England to absolve Mary's subjects from their sin of heresy and reconcile them with the Church of Rome.

The Spanish marriage proposal alarmed many Englishmen and there were widespread plans for a rising to force Mary to abandon her betrothal to Philip, but they were mishandled and only Kent rose, under Sir Thomas Wyatt in January 1554. Wyatt, with a following, succeeded in crossing Kingston Bridge to march on London, but he was routed, while the Queen stayed impassively at St James's Palace. Mary was convinced that her sister was in league with Wyatt and sent her to the Tower, but

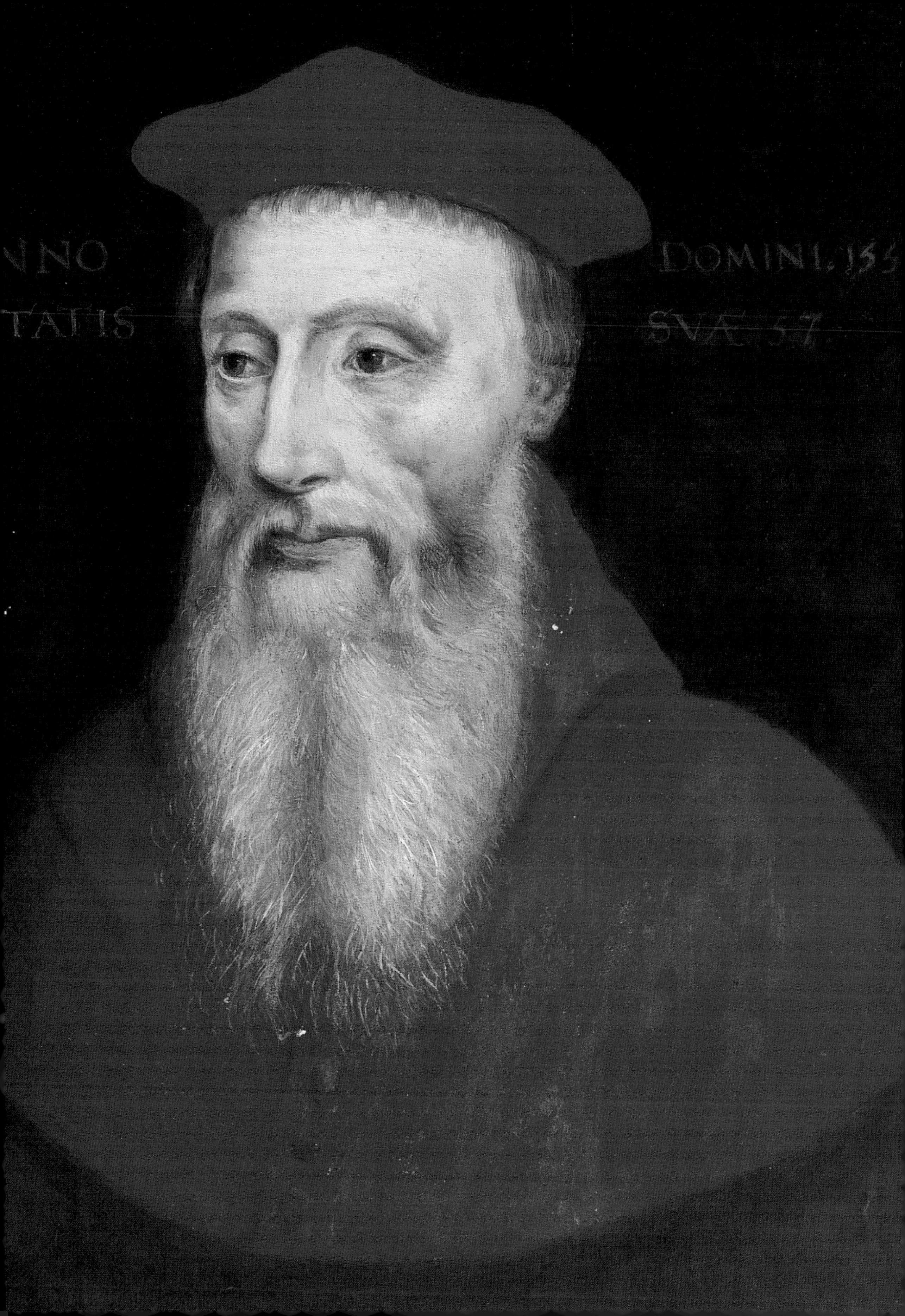
NNO
DOMINI. 15
TATIS
SVÆ 57

no evidence could be found to incriminate her so she was moved to Woodstock Palace to be out of the way when Philip arrived, for Elizabeth was the obvious focus for opponents to Mary's regime.

Philip and Mary married in Winchester Cathedral in July 1554 and proceeded to Hampton Court for their honeymoon. It was to Hampton that she returned the following May, convinced she was pregnant. Midwives were engaged and announcements of the happy event were prepared, ready signed, with blanks left for the sex and the date, to send to foreign courts. The weeks passed, yet no child was delivered: Mary had mistaken the symptoms of dropsy for signs of pregnancy. So desperately did she want a child, for its own sake quite apart from the need to maintain the Catholic succession, that next year there was a plot at court to pass off a suppositious prince, though it never reached her own ears.

Mary Tudor felt deserted by Philip, whose sole interest in marrying her had been to secure England's support for his continental designs.

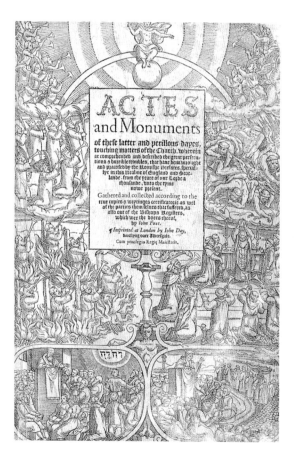

The title page of John Foxe's *Actes and Monuments*. Foxe's book, often known as the 'Book of Martyrs', describes the burning of prominent Protestant supporters during the reign of Mary I.

Besides Spain, he now had the government of the Netherlands, Milan and Naples assigned to him by his father, Charles V, who was abdicating, and there was the growing problem of the Spanish Empire in the New World. Philip could not believe it when Parliament refused to have him crowned 'King of England'.

His Queen was sure the ill-success of their marriage was due to divine vengeance – a punishment for the heresies still practised in England – and so the fires of Smithfield began. Hooper, the deprived Bishop of Gloucester, was burnt at the stake in February 1555 and later in the year Archbishop Cranmer and Bishops Ridley and Latimer followed him. Many clergy and lay folk who would not turn from their Protestantism escaped to Geneva or Zurich to await safer, saner times, but the militants who remained faced persecution and risked death. Their heroism is enshrined in John Foxe's 'Book of Martyrs' as his *Acts and Monuments* soon became known. The burnings provoked utter disillusionment with Mary's regime and her leading minister Cardinal Pole.

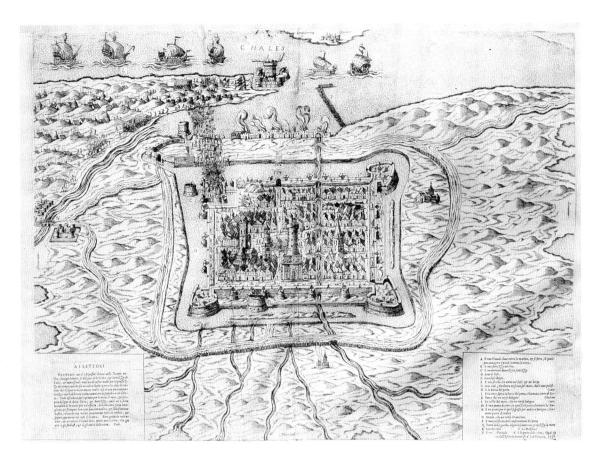

England had entered the war with France as Spain's ally and despite an early success at St Quentin, there came in January 1558 the great national disaster of the loss of Calais, England's last possession in France to which it had hung tenaciously since the end of the Hundred Years' War. Mary bore the brunt of the blame and she knew that instead of raising the stature of England by her marriage to Philip, she had brought national prestige to the lowest point in memory.

Mary's illness became progressively worse and Philip's absence caused her to turn to her step-sister and achieve in her final months some measure of reconciliation. Elizabeth was at Hatfield when Mary died at St James's on 17 November 1558. It was in the Chapel Royal at St James's that Mary's heart and bowels were buried, though her corpse was laid to rest at Westminster Abbey. Perhaps this symbolises her torn interests. Half-Spanish by birth and married to a Spaniard, she never understood her native people.

Spanish engraving of Calais prior to the capture of the town by French forces under the command of the Duke of Guise in 1558.

ELIZABETH I *r.* 1558–1603

THE DAUGHTER OF HENRY VIII and Anne Boleyn came into her inheritance on 17 November 1558, a day to be marked by celebrations even after the close of her long reign some forty-four years later. The 'crown imperial' was hers of right, and for this she had never known a mother's love, had carried the stigma of bastardy, had faced the terrors of suspicion when Somerset and Northumberland ruled for her young brother Edward and had endured the peril of the Tower and the ignominy of exile at Woodstock in her sister Mary's reign. Elizabeth had triumphed over endless difficulties and at the age of twenty-five learned at Hatfield that her reign had begun: 'This is the Lord's doing; it is marvellous in our eyes,' she quoted from the Psalms. Throughout the land there was rejoicing; bonfires were lit in thankfulness that the burnings at Smithfield were over, tables were brought into the streets of London for folk to 'eat and drink and make merry for the new Queen', and in York when the accession proclamation was read, her name was greeted as a true sovereign 'of no mingled blood of Spaniard, or stranger, but born mere English here among us'. She saw it as her mission to unite a divided people and she came to embody a truly national consciousness with such success that she gave her name to an age.

Her early years had been spent chiefly at Hunsdon and Hatfield manors under the care of Lady Bryan, but when she was four Catherine Champernowne was appointed her governess and quickly won her confidence. Catherine gave her a remarkable grasp of languages and classical scholarship; by the time she was six one courtier reckoned that if her formal education ceased forthwith 'she will prove of no less honour and womanhood than shall be seen her father's daughter'.

Opposite: Queen Elizabeth I, painted by Marcus Gheeraerts. This is unusual among surviving portraits of the queen as it shows the ravages of age – it was painted in 1595, when Elizabeth was sixty-two years old.

PROFES. IOANNES CHECUS EQUES AURATUS LINGUA GRÆ

Ingenium magni moderatus Principis exul
CHECVS, at inconstans in Pietate fuit. AB

The picture here set down
within this letter T.
A right doth shew the formes
of Tharlton vnto the shap
When hee in pleasant wise
the Counterfeit exprest
of Clowne w coate of russet
and shurtups w p reste, hem.

Whoe merry many mad,
when he appeard in sight.
The graue and wise as well as
at him did take delight, rud.

The partie nowe is gone,
and closlie clad in claye,
Of all the Iesters in the lande
he bare the praise awaie.

Now hath he plaid his pte,
and sure he is of this.
If hem Christe did dieso lure
with him in lasting blis.

An illustration portraying Richard Tarleton, Elizabeth's favourite clown.

Though she saw little of him Elizabeth was devoted to King Henry and later on would revere his memory for what he had achieved in Church and State. At last, after he married Catherine Parr in 1543, the three royal children were brought to court for long periods, so with a room at Whitehall Palace next door to the Queen's she felt she had a settled home. Catherine encouraged her studies so she now had Greek lessons from John Cheke, learned Italian from Battisti Castiglioni and, to her father's delight, made excellent progress on the virginals. Godly learning in the Erasmian tradition was varied by riding, archery and dancing, in all of which Elizabeth excelled. There was much practical relevance in the curriculum for a future ruler, though at the time no one expected the Princess to become more than the consort of a foreign sovereign.

The earliest portrait shows a pale-faced girl of thirteen, with auburn hair and innocent eyes, regal and confident in her bearing, seriously

Opposite: Portrait of Sir John Cheke, who was responsible for teaching Greek to the young Elizabeth.

reflecting on the book she is holding. Those final years of Henry's reign were perhaps the most peaceful of times. He had been the one constant factor in her life and once he died there would be endless difficulties for her. The Act of Succession had settled the Crown in turn on Edward, Mary and Elizabeth and although Henry had confirmed this in his will, he went on to provide for the remote possibility of all three of his children dying childless, in which case the Crown should descend to the heirs of his younger sister Mary (the Suffolk line) instead of the heirs of his elder sister Margaret, who had married James IV of Scotland in 1503 (the Stuart line). In the event Elizabeth was to override his preference, just as Edward Seymour, Earl of Hertford, immediately abrogated the dying King's plans for a Council of Regents by seizing power himself.

Elizabeth stayed with her step-mother in Chelsea but soon the Protector's brother, Lord Admiral Seymour, had intruded on their household to marry the Queen Dowager and flirt with the fourteen-year-old Princess. He would barge into her bedroom to tickle her and snatch kisses, but for all his charm he became repulsive to her and she was relieved when Catherine sent her to stay at Cheshunt, where she had the company of 'Kat' Ashley (her governess had married John Ashley, the friend of Roger Ascham). Soon Ascham himself became her tutor, extending her scholarship by his method of 'double translation'. Later, Ascham remarked on her industry, prodigious memory and modesty. She was not entirely free from Thomas Seymour: when Catherine Parr died in childbed he was indeed free to marry her. Rumours were rife, but the Princess dismissed the topic – 'it was but a London news'. The Admiral's plans to overturn his brother were tumbled and he was sent to the Tower. In the investigations Mistress Ashley and Thomas Parry, the Princess's cofferer, were themselves examined in the Tower to wring from them any incriminating evidence, while Elizabeth was cross-questioned by Sir Robert Tyrwhit who was amazed at her circumspect answers. For a time she was denied Kat Ashley's service but made such a fuss that the Council relented. The list of treasons alleged against Seymour, which sent him to the block, included craftily attempting to marry Elizabeth; long afterwards she spoke of him as 'a man of much wit and very little judgement'. She survived by steering clear of politics under Northumberland. Despite her Protestantism she was relieved at the failure of the attempt to place Lady Jane Grey on the throne, for the establishment of the Suffolk line would have ruled out her own right to succeed, and with Mary's accession she became heir apparent.

Opposite: Robert Dudley, Earl of Leicester, was one of Elizabeth I's most passionate admirers, known to her as 'sweet Robin'. He remained devoted to her until his death a month after the victory against the Armada in 1588.

Elizabeth 1 enjoying a picnic with her courtiers, from the 1576 book *The Noble Art of Venerie and Hunting* by George Turberbille.

With Mary's re-establishment of Catholicism and betrothal to Philip of Spain, the real test began for Elizabeth. Opposition to Mary naturally focused on her sister, who was popular, and she had to be on her guard to avoid entanglement in the plots woven about her. Suspected of complicity in Wyatt's revolt, she was summoned from Ashridge to court and, as she was ill, was brought in a litter by easy stages to Whitehall Palace where Mary refused to see her. After a month she was taken by barge to the Tower in terror of being quietly put out of the way, but she bravely told her warders she was no traitor 'but as true a woman to the Queen's Majesty as any'. Mary suspected much and could not believe Elizabeth was being frank when she swore that though Wyatt might have written to her, 'on my faith I never received any from him'. Yet since the Queen had no evidence to send her for trial she had no justification for confining her, even though the political situation required her to be under close surveillance. At last after eight weeks in the Tower she was moved to Woodstock in Oxfordshire in the custody of a stiff-necked Norfolk squire, Sir Henry Bedingfield. Here Elizabeth remained for ten months, to all intents a prisoner, while Mary married Philip and Cardinal Pole reconciled England with the Church of Rome.

At Woodstock there were pin-pricking restrictions about her books, about letter-writing and about her devotions. When she was ill, Mary refused her request for a royal physician to attend her and said an Oxford doctor would do just as well. This brought a characteristic outburst – 'I am not minded to make any stranger privy to the state of my body, but commit it to God.' The Queen gave way and sent Dr Owen to her, and his treatment reduced the swellings in her face and arms. She kept up her spirits by her duel of wits with Bedingfield and remained ambivalent about her conversion to Catholicism; some said she only heard Mass daily 'to give the impression that she had changed her religion. However she is too clever to get herself caught.' At last in April

1555 she was allowed to return to court and though she stubbornly denied there had been any fault in her behaviour, which angered Mary as it made plain that Elizabeth felt she had been wrongfully punished, there came a reconciliation between the half-sisters when the Princess unreservedly professed her undying loyalty. For the rest of the reign she remained chiefly at Hatfield, with Sir Thomas Pope, who proved a much more cultivated and endearing guardian than Bedingfield. Proposals for her hand had come thick and fast, from Habsburg Princes, from the Duke of Savoy and from the King of Sweden's son, but Elizabeth said 'she had no wish to marry'. In the summer of 1557 Queen and Princess kept midsummer together at Richmond and later in the year Mary paid a state visit to Hatfield. In her last illness Mary agreed with the Spanish ambassador and her Council that only Elizabeth could succeed her and sent word imploring her to maintain the old faith.

Engraving depicting Elizabeth on board a warship. Although she did not continue her father's expansionist policies, Elizabeth was committed to the recovery of Calais.

As Queen, indeed, the most urgent problem was the religious settlement. From the beginning Elizabeth was determined to avoid the extremes of both her brother's and her sister's reigns, so that her people could live together in unity and concord and she strove hard to establish a Church which was broadly based with a doctrine sufficiently elastic to satisfy the vast majority of her subjects. This middle way naturally antagonised the Protestant exiles returning from Geneva and Zurich who had greeted Elizabeth as Deborah, the restorer of Israel, and hoped that the doctrine embodied in the 1552 Prayer Book would be reintroduced, but episcopacy abolished, for they had drunk deeply at the wells of Calvinism. Such partisan views were anathema to the Queen and, despite the pressure of Protestants in Parliament, the *via media* was to be pursued. She would not, she said 'open windows in men's souls'. Outward conformity by attendance at church of a Sunday was enough; if men chose also to hear the Roman Mass privately or to attend a sectarian

meeting there would be no harm done. Alas, because she was both Queen and Supreme Governor of the Church of England, 'nonconformity' would come to be interpreted as 'disloyalty' to the regime and after 1570, when the Pope had the effrontery to issue a bull deposing her and absolving her subjects from their allegiance, practising Catholics were turned into potential traitors. In a similar way the Puritan wing of Protestantism came to undermine royal authority. Under the pressure of political events Elizabeth's ideal of a golden mean could not be achieved, but there is no denying her abhorrence of persecution and her fundamental dislike of extremes.

From the first Elizabeth placed exceptional trust in William Cecil, who had helped to administer her properties as Princess, and he was destined to serve her devotedly until his death in 1598, first as Principal Secretary, then as Lord Treasurer – a remarkable partnership. Matthew Parker, whom she selected as Archbishop of Canterbury, fulfilled all her expectations of him in moulding the Church of England, though she never approved of his having a wife. These two men were links with the past: Cecil's grandfather had fought for her grandfather at Bosworth, while Parker had connections with the Boleyns.

At the outset of the reign de Feria, the Spanish ambassador, had noted that Elizabeth was 'much attached to the people and is very confident that they take her part'. Her popularity was indeed most obvious during the festivities accompanying the coronation on 15 January 1559, a date which the astrologer John Dee had helped her to select. The post of Lord High Steward of England at the coronation went to Henry, Earl of Arundel, a widower who fancied his chances of becoming consort. Another English candidate was Sir William Pickering, a diplomat whose swagger upset everyone, but there was no shortage of foreign princes offering their hands – Philip of Spain himself, the Duke of Holstein, Eric of Sweden and two Habsburg Archdukes. It was taken for granted in England and abroad that Elizabeth would marry and that marriage would solve the problem of the succession; her marriage and the succession were the twin topics on which Parliament continued to press her, to her extreme annoyance – they would never have dared to treat her father thus, she growled.

The problem of the succession was the more acute since, immediately on Mary's death, her cousin Mary Queen of Scots, wife of the Dauphin of France, had claimed to be rightful Queen of England in Elizabeth's place, and when the Dauphin succeeded to the throne as

Opposite: Mary Stuart, Queen of Scotland, cousin of Mary I. Supported by many Catholics, Mary sought to replace the Protestant Elizabeth as Queen of England.

Francis II in July 1559, England looked most vulnerable; never had the 'auld alliance' between Scotland and France been so menacing, for both were controlled by the Guise faction. That winter the English fought over the border as allies of the Protestant Lords of the Congregation to expel the French and, by the Treaty of Edinburgh which followed, the Scots fully recognised Elizabeth's right to her throne and undertook that their own Queen, still in France, should relinquish her claim. The sudden death of Francis II in December 1560 increased Elizabeth's difficulties, since Mary would now reside in Scotland. Mary consistently refused to ratify the Treaty of Edinburgh, unless Elizabeth would name her as her successor, and Mary's search for another husband, in England and on the continent, further aggravated the matter. The two Queens, enemies to the end, would never meet each other.

Elizabeth caught smallpox in 1562 and seemed near to death. Ministers discussed who might succeed her, which was no longer an academic question, especially as there were 'nearly as many different opinions as there were councillors present'. When the Queen recovered she said that in case of a like emergency, Lord Robert Dudley should be made Protector of the realm. Dudley, Northumberland's fifth son, had been appointed Master of the Horse and had come to high favour by April 1559; he was so much with the Queen that men said that had he not already a wife Elizabeth would have married him, and exaggerated tales of their relationship were related in foreign courts. Then Dudley's wife, Amy Robsart, died in suspicious circumstances and though the coroner's inquest cleared Lord Robert – he was with the Queen at Windsor at the time – the tragedy at Cumnor made all the difference to the question of marriage. Dudley was in any case too controversial a figure in personality and politics to take as a husband without dividing her court and people, though she remained emotionally tied to 'sweet Robin' till his death. The request that he might become Protector if anything happened to her indicates the strength of their special relationship. 'The Queen would like everyone to be in love with her', commented a shrewd ambassador, 'but I doubt whether she will ever be in love with anyone enough to marry him.' Though there were to be other suitors from abroad, notably the Archduke Charles and then the French Duke of Alençon, Dudley long cherished the hope of marrying the Queen, nor was he the only Englishman with this ambition.

Christopher Hatton, who had caught her eye at a masque by his fine dancing, became one of the corps of Gentlemen Pensioners, her

Opposite: Sir Christopher Hatton was another of Elizabeth's favourites, author of ardent love letters and rewarded for his loyalty with the Bishop of Ely's house in Holborn and the post of Lord Chancellor.

TANDEM SI

personal bodyguard of which in 1572 he became Captain. While she nicknamed Robert Dudley 'Eyes', Hatton became 'Lids' and wrote her passionate love letters: 'To serve you is heaven, but to lack you is more than hell's torment.' He wept when she spurned him and vowed to stay celibate for her sake, dreaming of the idyll which might have been, and she loved him for it. She forced the Bishop of Ely to give him his house in Holborn, while the favourite built Holdenby House in his native Lincolnshire as a 'shrine' for her. He was to become Lord Chancellor. There developed a curious bond between Dudley, Hatton and also Heneage through their rival devotion to the Queen, but none of them could stand the outsider, Walter Raleigh, who made his début at court in 1581.

Though the society in which she lived at court was essentially masculine, Elizabeth succeeded in dominating it, evoking a genuine emotional response from courtiers in general because she was a woman as well as a queen. She charmed those about her into participating in the sophisticated allegorical fantasy of the Virgin Queen, contriving to live out a mystical romance on a public stage. The musicians and poets praised her as Fair Oriana or as the immortal shepherdess of a pastoral and the older she grew the more she delighted in the cult. Her household resembled a large family, often on the move between residences, and as a family it had its feuds, when factions formed around strong personalities. It was not out of malice that Elizabeth opposed her maids of honour's plans to marry, but because marriages broke up her own family circle. Like her father Elizabeth wanted her court to become a great cultural centre, an academy where scholars, musicians and artists could find fellowship and patronage, although she was not prepared to spend as freely as Henry VIII. Musicians such as William Byrd fared much better than the poets, and Edmund Spenser failed to find a post at court even when he had dedicated *The Faerie Queene* to his sovereign.

To solve the problem of Mary of Scotland, Elizabeth had suggested that Mary might marry her own Dudley, whom she created Earl of Leicester. Mary, however, had set her heart on Lord Darnley, descended from Queen Margaret's second marriage with the Earl of Angus. The fact that Darnley was an English subject made him even more unsuitable in Elizabeth's eyes, yet in July 1565 their marriage took place. 'King Darnley' fathered the future James I and VI, but soon showed himself a worthless sot and he was murdered at Kirk o'-Field, probably on the Earl of Bothwell's order. Next month Mary married Bothwell, provoking the

Opposite: The dramatic rise in favour of the dashing and handsome Walter Raleigh, shown here in an anonymous portrait, deeply annoyed the triumvirate of Elizabeth's closest confidants, Dudley, Hatton and Heneage.

Lords of the Covenant to arms; they defeated Bothwell at Carberry Hill and forced Mary to abdicate. In May 1568, however, she escaped from Lochleven Castle, to throw herself on Elizabeth's mercy, but the Queen decided she had no alternative but to keep her in close custody. Unwillingly she found herself acting as arbiter between Mary and her subjects and while she could never forgive a claimant to her throne, she would not lightly sacrifice an anointed queen to rebellious subjects.

Mary's presence in England provoked the Northern Rebellion of 1569 in which the Earls of Northumberland and Westmorland aimed to restore Catholicism and place Mary on the throne. The rebels were defeated by Hunsdon, the Queen's cousin, but another cousin, Thomas Howard, fourth Duke of Norfolk, was found to be deeply implicated in the rising and in 1572 was executed for his share in the Ridolfi conspiracy. Elizabeth would have preferred to pardon him, but Cecil pointed out to her the inexorable logic of statecraft. Thereafter a further series of conspiracies were planned by Catholics to carry out the papal bull deposing Elizabeth; all hinged on foreign aid and saw the Queen's death as a preliminary to Mary Stuart's accession. In this atmosphere of plot and counterplot Elizabeth showed remarkable courage and forbearance, trying hard to reduce the severity of the Draconian laws against her Catholic subjects. Francis Walsingham, now Secretary of State, longed for her to take a positive role in opposing the forces of the Counter Reformation in Europe by supporting the Dutch Protestants against Philip of Spain and intervening on the side of the Huguenots in the French religious wars, but she was anxious to be at peace with her neighbours, hating the waste and inhumanity of war, even if she profited by the marauding of Hawkins and Drake against Spanish possessions in the New World. In 1572, however, England at last found an ally in France and to preserve this alliance Elizabeth undertook a protracted courtship of the Duke of Alençon, throwing herself into the role of lover with gay abandon.

Francois Alençon was half her age and diminutive beside her, yet he had remarkable charm and she fell for his flattery. During 1579 it seemed as if she would really marry him, but there was a Puritan outcry against the Duke's 'unprince-like, French kind of wooing'. The discovery that Leicester had secretly married the beautiful Lettice Knollys, while still protesting his undying love for Elizabeth, would almost have driven her into Alençon's arms, had it not been for Protestant fervour; the match eventually failed, as the Habsburg marriage negotiations had also

THE ENDVR
WORDE ETH
OF THE FOR
LORD EVER

SVPERSTICION

IDOLATRY

ALL FLESHE
IS GRASSE

FEYNED
HOLINE

Habes Lector candide, fortiß, ac inuictiß Ducis Draeck ad Viuum Imaginem qui toto terrarum orbe, duorum annorum, et mensium decem spatio, Zephiris fauen= tibus circumducto, Angliam sedes proprias. 4. Cal. Octobr. anno á partu Virgi= nis 1580 reuisit cum antea portu soluißet Id. Decem: anni, 1577.

foundered in 1567, because the potential bride-groom was a Catholic. Her head overcame her heart and she let Alençon go, but by now she was in her late forties and knew that it was her last chance of marriage and children.

Her depression was saved by the arrival of Walter Raleigh, a west countryman of singular wit and gallantry, who praised her in verse. Leicester's nose was soon out of joint and Hatton in utter despair, for Raleigh's rise to favour was meteoric. She was truly fascinated by Raleigh and fed on his adoration; only he would have tried to plant a colony in North America and name it Virginia, after his Queen. Yet eventually, when he realised that she would never marry him and found happiness with Bess Throckmorton, the Queen was furious and banished them both from court.

War with Spain loomed nearer as Walsingham's agents pieced together plans for Philip II's enterprise against England, and then Mary Queen of Scots was found to be person-ally committed in the Babington Plot against the Queen's life. Elizabeth hesitated long over sending Mary to her execution at Fotheringhay and then blamed it on her offi-cials. Burghley (as Cecil had become) was in disgrace and for a time feared the Tower.

Already, following the murder of William the Silent, she had been per-suaded to send an army under Leicester to fight against the Spanish in the Netherlands, though she refused to accept the sovereignty of the Dutch people. Drake and the seadogs, flushed with their successes in the Caribbean, urged open war with Spain, but still Elizabeth held back, preferring negotiation to fighting. Drake's raid on Cadiz postponed the sailing of the Armada for a year, but at last in August 1588 the great Spanish fleet was in the Channel, endeavouring to gain command of the Straits of Dover to launch a full-scale invasion.

In this moment of crisis Elizabeth was superb. Against her councillors' wishes she went down to Tilbury Camp to exhort the troops

Queen Elizabeth I with Burghley and Wolsingham, two of her closest advisors.

Opposite: Portrait of Sir Francis Drake made in about 1580. The globe in the background commemorates Drake's circumnavigation of the world, undertaken between 1577 and 1580.

Den VIII february werde onthalst Maria

Mary Queen of Scots's execution at Fotheringhay Castle, which followed the discovery of her involvement in the Babington Plot against Elizabeth's life.

under Leicester at the very moment when it was feared an invasion would be attempted. 'Let tyrants fear. I have always so behaved myself that, under God, I have placed my chiefest strength and goodwill in the loyal hearts and goodwill of my subjects … I know I have but the body of a weak and feeble woman, but I have the heart and stomach of a King.' She spoke for England.

The Armada, scattered from Calais Roads by the fireships, was driven into the North Sea, to find its way home by the north of Scotland and Ireland. The Spanish defeat did not succeed in bringing Philip II to his knees, but it put fresh heart into the cause of Protestantism in Europe, especially in Holland. Through divine intervention, men said, the Colossus of Spain had at last been stayed and

Elizabeth was the heroine of the hour. None then predicted that the war would outlast the Queen's reign.

Leicester's death the following month soured the fruits of victory. She locked herself in her room and would see no one, so that her councillors ordered her door to be broken down, fearing for her safety. The intensity of her feeling for Leicester was revealed only after her own death, when in a little casket by her bed was found among her treasured keepsakes the letter that Leicester had written to her from Rycote the night before he died; to it had been added her own inscription in a shaky hand: 'His last letter'.

Old age brought its harsh losses. Soon she was being called to the bedside of Christopher Hatton at Ely Place to feed him 'with cordial broths' as he lay dying, then Walsingham went and finally old Burghley, who had triumphed by bringing in his second son Robert Cecil to

The 'Danger Averted' gold medal incorporated a portrait of Elizabeth and was struck to celebrate the defeat of the Spanish Armada in 1588.

The most noble ROBERT
Earle of Essex and Ewe, Earle
Marshall of England, Vicount He-
reford and Bourgcher, Lord Ferres
of Chartley, L. Bourgcher and
Louayn, and her Maiesties
lieutenant, and Gouernour generall
of the Kingdome of Irland. 1601.

HIC TVVS ILLE COMES GENEROSA ESSEXIA NOSTRIS
QVEM QVAM GAVDEMVS REBVS ADESSE DVCEM.

Six engraved Armada playing cards from the late seventeenth century, demonstrating strong anti-Catholic feeling.

share his power. The series of 'Armada portraits' and the splendid painting of Elizabeth standing on the map of England (1592) concealed the ravages time had made on her face and figure. Marvellous in jewels and ruff, Gloriana was almost sixty, and had resorted to an auburn wig to hide her thinning hair, and a liberal use of cosmetics. Still the masquerade went on and the final act was dominated by Leicester's step-son, Robert, Earl of Essex, a handsome youth who fancied himself as a general and looked to the Queen to retrieve him from financial ruin. Robert Cecil outwitted him in Council, yet Essex banked all on success against the Irish rebels.

He came home in defiance of the Queen's orders and gambled on saving himself by his charm, but she had decided to teach him a long-overdue lesson and she refused to underwrite his vast debts. In 1601 he drifted into conspiracy, aiming at the throne himself, but his revolt was

Opposite: An engraving by Boissard of Robert, Earl of Essex, who relied too heavily on Elizabeth's indulgence and patronage and was eventually executed for treason after an unsuccessful attempt to seize the throne.

The Chariott drawne by foure Horses vpon which charret stood the Coffin couered w:th purple Veluett and vpon that the representation, The Canopy borne by six Knight:

footemen.

easily suppressed and Essex was executed for treason. Elizabeth reckoned he had as little judgement as Thomas Seymour, two generations back.

That year she addressed her last Parliament and her touch was as sure as ever. She had always taken great care with her speeches from the days of her first Parliaments, but now she delivered what posterity called her 'golden speech', because it epitomised the relationship of sovereign and people in a golden age of monarchy which effectively ended with her death. Being Queen, she told them, was a glorious thing, but it was her people's loyalty and love that mattered: 'There will never Queen sit in my seat with more zeal to my country … And though you have had, and may have, many Princes more mighty and wise, sitting in this state, yet you never had, or shall have, any that will be more careful and loving.'

Elizabeth had never named her successor and even at the last would not do so, for she knew that the careful Cecil was discreetly planning for James VI of Scotland, the son of Mary Stuart and Darnley, to enter upon the seat of kings on her demise. After Christmas 1602 she began to feel most frail and six weeks later fell ill while at Richmond. The Insomnia she suffered was far worse to bear than sickness and it increased her melancholy. Her work of 'having brought up, even under her wing, a nation that was almost begotten and born under her' (as Thomas Dekker put it) was over. She died on 24 March 1603, the last of the Tudors and the greatest of queens.

The funeral cortège of Elizabeth I, last of the Tudor monarchs, from a contemporary painting by William Camden.

Opposite: Painting depicting Elizabeth defying the wishes of her advisers and visiting Tilbury to inspire the forces assembled to meet the formidable Spanish Armada.

INDEX

PICTURE CREDITS

The Bridgeman Art Library, London: endpapers. pages 24, 27, 29, 30, 34, 36, 37, 39, 42, 54–55, 60, 62–63, 64, 75, 77, 83, 88, 92–93, 97, 99, 100
Sotheby's Picture Library: pages 2, 17
theartarchive: pages 8, 40–41, 45, 46, 48–49, 53, 65, 81, 82
Weidenfeld & Nicolson Archives; pages 18, 31, 38, 70, 71, 72, 74, 78, 79, 87, 91, 95, 96, 98, 101

AKG London: pages 21, 56, 69, 85
Sotheby's Picture Library: pages 33, 67, 73
Topham Picturepoint: page 43
Christie's Images: pages 50, 59
Hulton Getty: page 94